Following

Reflections for Your Journey with Jesus

Alan Amavisca

BARCLAY PRESS

Newberg, OR 97132

Following

Reflections for Your Journey with Jesus

©2021 by Alan Amavisca

Barclay Press, Inc.
Newberg, Oregon
www.barclaypress.com

Illustrations by Deborah F. Correa

Printed in the United States of America.

ISBN 978-1-59498-080-0

To Barbara:

Wife, friend, and companion on the journey.
Your devotion to Jesus inspires my own.

In Memorial:

Lori Anderson
(1964–2019)

Friend, co-worker, and wise woman
of God.
Lori created the layout for Entre Nous
And edited my writing with grace.
You are missed.

Contents

Foreword

Whether you are a local church pastor, a Sunday school teacher, an usher, a missionary, or a person wanting to work for the Lord but not sure just how you fit in, this book of reflections by Alan Amavisca is for you. It will inspire, motivate, and encourage you.

While this book is geared toward Christian leaders and workers, Alan's understanding of the church recognizes that God calls each of us to some kingdom task. Theologians call that "the priesthood of believers." It means that whatever the size of your current arena of service, you are one of the readers for whom Alan wrote this book.

These reflections flow from Alan's years of experience in Christian ministry. After fourteen years as a Quaker missionary in Guatemala, Alan worked for ten years as the pastor of missions at Friends Church Yorba Linda and nine as the director of missions and church planting for the Evangelical Friends Church Southwest. For five years he has led an interdenominational ministry (North County Project) that makes disciples among the unchurched and also equips and encourages emerging leaders to reach out in the North Orange County area. As part of his leadership of this ministry, Alan has sent out a weekly newsletter to his teammates, clients, and supporters. This newsletter includes a reflection based on Scripture, intended to encourage those actively engaged in the hard work of being salt and light in their context. After many expressed their appreciation for the encouragement and suggested, repeatedly, that he publish the biblical reflections, Alan decided to take on the task that has resulted in this book. All these reflections are experience-based and field-tested.

Each reflection begins with Scripture, then brings the biblical context forward into our twenty-first-century reality, challenges readers with some new insight, and ends with a query that motivates personal application. The topics cover the call to ministry, qualities we as workers need to let God grow in us, biblical strategies for service, lifestyle issues, and the temptations and struggles common to those who follow Jesus. They reflect on what it means to be the living church in our present context of conflict. But— and this is crucial—all these reflections are centered in a deep spirituality that puts a relationship with Jesus first. It's work and service from a base of faith and rest.

Many of the reflections focus on the place of the church, and the Christian worker, in the surrounding society. One challenges us to show our children and grandchildren "how to live proactively and biblically in a world that sometimes disappoints and occasionally turns toxic." Another centers on civility in the public arena, asking, "Am I a voice for grace and humility and wisdom from above? What can I do to bring a reconciling witness and meaningful solution to the public debate?" Another reflection questions the church's response to the culture in an age of rage, asking, "Am I reacting to the world's raging or proactively reflecting Jesus in the midst of it?"

I could continue with many examples, but better that you read these reflections for yourself. You can read them one at a time, moving in order through the book, or choosing according to current interest and need. The book will be especially helpful as a devotional resource for staff/team/committee meetings, giving both ministerial focus and personal encouragement.

Let this book of reflections become God's tool in maturing you in a life of service.

Nancy Thomas
Quaker writer, poet, retired "official"
missionary (ongoing "real" missionary)

Introduction

Barbara and I began our foray into formal ministry in 1981 when we were confirmed as missionaries to Guatemala with Evangelical Friends Church Southwest. A few months after our arrival in Guatemala City, we received a visit from the Southwest superintendent at that time, Earl Geil. Earl made it a practice to read the Bible several times a year, and during that visit he inspired me to embrace this discipline as well.

For the past thirty-seven years, I have maintained the practice—noting any meaningful lessons in my journal. In later years I would choose one each week to develop into a reflection. I have selected the fifty-nine reflections in this book from among those I have written over the past twelve years for my weekly newsletter, *Entre Nous*.

My original audience consisted of missionaries and church planters, which later expanded to pastors and church staff members. Over the years the community continued growing and now most of my readers minister bivocationally. By day they sell coffee, work in hospitals, run businesses, or practice law; off-hours they evangelize, disciple, elder, or teach.

So while I have tried to capture how the scriptures have impacted me in my daily reading, I have always sought to share that impact as one minister to another as we follow Jesus together.

I pray these reflections encourage you to press on and press deeper into him as you live out your own kingdom service.

Stay Rooted

Blessed is the one who perseveres under trial because,
having stood the test, that person will receive the crown
of life that the Lord has promised to those who love
him.
—James 1:12

What a great reminder with which to begin any new
endeavor. In the face of the inevitable adversities, relational dramas, or personal heartbreaks we will face in
the course of a new project—or new year—we have
an assurance: God will bless us if we hold fast.

"If we hold fast." This phrase sounds ominous.
One could interpret James 1:12 to mean that the
outcome is in question. When we are in the midst of
fierce conflict or overwhelming grief, the likelihood of
survival often feels doubtful. But two promises give
me hope when storms shake my foundations.

The first promise is found in Psalm 1. This psalm
begins with the same phrase James uses, "Blessed is
the one," and then goes on to tell us why: "[Their]
delight is in the law of the Lord," and they meditate
on God's law both day and night. The psalmist then

explains that such a one is like "a tree planted by streams of water, which yields its fruit in season . . . whatever they do prospers."

The psalmist invites us to make a point of abiding in God's word, allowing God's word—not the world—to shape our souls and perspective. As we abide in Scripture and allow God's Spirit to abide in us and bring the written Word to life, we can draw great strength from the struggle.

The second promise is a reminder of God's grace: "No temptation has overtaken you except what is common to mankind. And God is faithful; he will not let you be tempted beyond what you can bear. But when you are tempted, he will also provide a way out so that you can endure it" (1 Corinthians 10:13). In other words, no matter how hard the challenge or savage the battle, we know God will not allow us to find ourselves trapped in a circumstance that is beyond what we can handle. And remember, often God's provision for trials comes in the form of friends, family members, or the church body. We do not need to face adversity alone.

Rooted in God's Word, attentive to God's Spirit, confident in God's mediating influence when we go through trials, we can press through the storms that accompany any new circumstance, like trees planted by streams of water. Not a bad reminder as we wade into the unknown!

Where have I sunk my "roots"?

Call and Betrayal

How long, Lord, must I call for help, but you do not
listen? Or cry out to you, "Violence!" but you do not
save? ... The wicked hem in the righteous,
so that justice is perverted.
—Habakkuk 1:2, 4b

When I served as mission and church planting
director, people regularly asked me to explain my job.
I told them that my primary responsibility was to try
and talk people out of doing ministry. That always
earned a quizzical glance! I would then explain that
the person I was interviewing had to convince me
they had a strong sense of calling, because ministry
can be so painful and costly. In fact, in my experience,
sometimes the *only* reason one stays with ministry is
a clear sense of mission to a place or people. In Stan
Leach's words, "The call is everything." I agree.

In one particular conversation, the other person followed up my answer with a question no one
had asked me before: "What is the hardest part
about ministry?" I was surprised how quickly I

responded—perhaps it was because I had just read Habakkuk. "Betrayal," I replied.

As soon as I said the word, a list of common betrayals came to mind. First, when a couple goes into ministry and one does not share the call (or at least a willingness to affirm God's call on their spouse), the results can be devastating: The spouse in ministry betrays their partner for the work or another. Or the supporting spouse checks out and later grows cold to God, or marriage, or life in general. In either case the loss of shared purpose within marriage ultimately forces them to step away from ministry.

Perhaps equally painful is the experience of a ministry team member turning on you—either working behind your back to destroy your reputation or else building alliances against you. It may be a case of jealousy or ambition (Gene Edward's book, *Tale of Three Kings*, is a must-read on this subject), but if you don't have a strong sense of call, such a blow can prompt you to give up.

Then there is the disciple you have invested in heavily who goes rogue (even Paul experienced this—2 Timothy 1:15) or simply decides to become part of another church. The latter is possibly the hardest to process, because we want to work for the good of the kingdom, yet it is hard not to consider "your" hours wasted. In either case we find that our love and care were not enough to carry the relationship, and that hurts.

However, the toughest "betrayal" is when we feel that God has gone silent . . . or turned on us. Then it seems only logical to despair like Habakkuk. Without a clear sense of calling, we would likely remain in the wilderness steeped in the bitterness of God's abandonment.

That is why the call is everything, whether the betrayal is real or perceived, human or divine. Habakkuk could despair, but he could not give up. In the midst of his railings against God, he never ceased listening to God: "Though the fig tree does not bud and there are no grapes on the vines, though the olive crop fails and the fields produce no food . . . yet I will rejoice in the Lord, I will be joyful in God my Savior" (Habakkuk 3:17a, 18).

The call is everything.

How would I summarize God's call on my life? How has knowing that helped me remain steady in my current ministry?

Go and Make Disciples

Then Jesus came to them and said, "All authority in heaven and on earth has been given to me. Therefore go and make disciples of all nations, baptizing them in the name of the Father and of the Son and of the Holy Spirit, and teaching them to obey everything I have commanded you. And surely I am with you always, to the very end of the age."
—Matthew 28:18–20

I had just finished reading the book of Matthew, and one fact loomed large: Jesus invested his life in a very small number of people. Who were they? James, John, and Peter, who were always with him; the other nine disciples, who were almost always with him; the seventy—men and women in whom he invested with some regularity. Jesus started a movement dependent upon twelve disciples and a few dozen of their friends. He had no plan B. I spoke on one occasion with a contractor friend about the high cost of construction. Our conversation reminded me that in Guatemala, where everything is built of block and rebar, about 25 percent of construction costs are below the ground. Before one ever sees a hint of a wall, workers must trench, lay massive amounts of rebar and concrete, run plumbing and electrical conduit, etc. It can be depressing when one has to write endless checks and seemingly has nothing to show for it! But the investment always pays off, because the foundation is everything. Take shortcuts there and you pay the price later.

The mission of the church is that simple: make disciples. That's the foundation of the church. Steep people in God's ways, model the message of Jesus, and encourage them to do the same as they reach out to others. Churches will form; communities will experience transformation.

At the end of the day, we either make disciples or we don't. A missionary once sent me this quote: "If you make disciples, you will always get the church, but if you make the church, you won't always get disciples."

Who are your disciples?

Unsafe Faith

As Jesus was walking beside the Sea of Galilee, he
saw two brothers, Simon called Peter and his brother
Andrew. They were casting a net into the lake, for they
were fishermen. "Come, follow me," Jesus said, "and I
will send you out
to fish for people."
—Matthew 4:18–19

"Is he—quite safe?" . . . "Safe?" said Mr. Beaver. . . .
"Who said anything about safe? Course he isn't safe.
But he's good. He's the King, I tell you."
—C. S. Lewis, *The Lion, the Witch
and the Wardrobe*

A few days ago, I tuned into a local Christian radio
station just in time to hear them declare themselves
as "safe for the whole family." Hmm. I wondered why
they chose that slogan; evidently they considered this
to be their greatest selling point. I changed stations.

Still, their tagline prompted me to wonder: When
did safety become a primary value for Jesus followers?
When Jesus called the disciples to leave their nets,
their farms, and their tax tables, He invited them into

a life of risk. I would love to hear a Christian radio station declare itself "the most dangerous place on your radio dial!" Wouldn't *that* be provocative?

For years I have heard people say the safest place to be is the center of God's will. *Spiritually speaking,* I suppose this statement is true. However, choosing to align ourselves with God's will does not guarantee protection from physical danger or harm. I prefer the way a veteran missionary explained God's call. He told me that his extended family (all Christians) had many reasons why he and his wife should stay home when they announced they were going to Panama as missionaries. He responded, "I would rather be in Panama in God's will than in Oregon out of God's will." No assumptions of divine protection from all harm, simply an acknowledgment that Jesus is worth following—anywhere.

Think again about the disciples. Jesus changed their professions; they risked everything on the conviction that he was indeed the Messiah. Remember: in the first century AD, the average laborer gathered and grew enough fish and grain to provide sufficient food for each day, with a tiny bit of extra. When the disciples chose to leave their nets, they literally put the lives of their families at risk.

They had concluded Jesus was worth it.

Safety? Not a clause in our "contract." This is what Jesus does tell us, however:

Blessed are those who are persecuted because of righteousness, for theirs is the kingdom of heaven. "Blessed are you when people insult you, persecute you and falsely say all kinds of evil against you because of me. Rejoice and be glad, because great is your reward in heaven, for in the same way they persecuted the prophets who were before you.

(Matthew 5:10–12).

Safe? No. But he's good.

Is there anywhere in my life I am resisting God's invitation to follow because it feels unsafe? What might the first step of obedience look like?

Guided by Prayer

And they went through the region of Phyrgia and
Galatia, having been forbidden by the Holy Spirit
to speak the word in Asia. . . . And a vision appeared
to Paul in the night. . . . And when Paul had seen the
vision, immediately we sought to go on into Macedonia.
—Acts 16:6, 9a, 10a (ESV)

Who would we be if the practice of intercessory prayer
shaped our leadership? How might it change the
dynamic between us and those we are leading if they
knew that we are regularly and routinely entering into
God's presence with the intent to speak and lead from
what transpires there?
—Ruth Haley Barton,
Strengthening the Soul of Your Leadership

It was a tough meeting, not because we were in
disagreement, but rather because we were wrestling
with an intractable problem. We agreed the obstacles
would require sustained intercession by God's
people—but as Americans we also recognized we
would rather do other things than pray.

My gravitational drift is toward planning
and solving more than praying my way through a

challenge. These are not wrong practices, but what is wrong is the temptation to rely on them and treat prayer as an afterthought—a closing three-minute exercise to a two-hour meeting.

Augustine said, "Pray as if everything depends on God, work as if it all depends on you." I think I do the second part well, but the prayer part?

Every time I read Acts, I'm reminded of the centrality of prayer in the life of the church: the Holy Spirit came down after a ten-day prayer meeting. The first Christians devoted themselves to prayer; they prayed in public spaces and in private. They prayed over decisions, the sick, the imprisoned, and the lost. The first formal mission was launched by a prayer meeting. And as these missionaries went out to proclaim the gospel, they prayed and obeyed: Why not Asia? Why Macedonia? God knew—that was enough.

I'm trying to reorder my life around this conviction, but bad habits die hard. Part of my goal is to make spaces for prayer throughout the day so that prayer becomes as natural as breathing. But I also want to listen more. Intercession is more than just clamoring and God taking notes; it is disciplined listening. And waiting. And heart transformation. And obeying. Prayer leads to action—the right action.

Paul's instruction to the Ephesians would serve us well:

And pray in the Spirit on all occasions with all kinds of prayers and requests. With this in mind, be alert and always keep on praying for all the Lord's people. Pray also for me, that whenever I speak, words may be given me so that I will fearlessly make known the mystery of the gospel.

(Ephesians 6:18-19)

What attitudes or activities interfere with further developing an unhurried and attentive prayer life? What steps can I take to change this?

Release and Receive

He must become greater; I must become less.
—John 3:30

[Jesus], being in the form of God, did not consider
equality with God something to be grasped.
—Philippians 2:6 (MEV)

John's disciples come looking for him, and they are
not happy. The new guy in town is cutting into their
"market share," and they want John to act. I wonder
what they thought when John responded the way he
did.

By letting go.

In ministry we often come face-to-face with a
fearful exchange. God asks us to release something; it
may be a key person on our team, a portion of our re-
serves—even funds we do not yet have. On occasion,
God may even ask us to release a ministry we have
exercised, or our reputation.

We balk. We recite a half-dozen reasons why this
exchange is a bad idea. But as we listen to ourselves,
our reasons sound increasingly silly, and we relent.

Love for God and for God's purposes displaces our fear; slowly we unfold our clutched hands and let go.

This is the moment. At the intersect of *releasing* what we held so precious and *receiving* what God has next, we experience fresh anointing for whatever God has in store for us, and in some unexpected fashion, God is glorified.

But it is hard to let go! The comfort, familiarity, and security we have acquired over time become entanglements that constrain our willingness to risk. The prospect of releasing what we know and enjoy for the unknown path of obedience fills our minds with anxiety and fear.

So Jesus shows us how. Jesus released all the prerogatives of deity in order to receive (take hold of) the Father's will. He released his identity as God the Son and received the role of Suffering Servant. He went all the way to death in the process. And to resurrection.

John the Baptist released his role as preparer of the way, released his disciples (John 1:35–37), released the crowds (John 3:25–26), and received the role of martyr and the recognition of Jesus as the greatest among us (Matthew 11:11).

Do I live with open hands before God? Am I willing to release what I have received from God in the past in order to receive whatever is next?

What Do You See?

When I consider your heavens, the work of your
fingers, the moon and the stars, which you have set in
place, what is mankind that you are mindful of them,
human beings that you care for them?
—Psalm 8:3–4

I came across an article in which the writer argued
for the impossibility of God, given the size and self-
sufficiency of the universe. Why would a God capable
of creating such a universe give a rip about one
species among many on a tiny planet on a minimal
star system that is casting about in one minor galaxy
among hundreds of millions of galaxies?

Fast-forward to my morning devotions a few days
later. I was reading Psalm 8, and when I came to verses
3 and 4, I thought, "Fascinating—the psalmist essentially asks the same question as the atheist!" Both acknowledged the enormity of the universe and the tiny
place of humans in the scheme of things. However,
whereas the latter decided no God of any meaningful magnitude would possibly care about such minor
critters, the psalmist came to another conclusion. No,

we are not meaningless; we are "a little lower than the angels" (v. 5). All of us—every single human being.

Funny, isn't it? Two people look at exactly the same canopy of stars, and one sees cold space, the other a fabulous Artist determined to engage us and draw us into relationship.

When I look at the stars, when I look under the bridges of my city, when I look in the mirror—what do I see?

Tradition

He replied, "Isaiah was right when he prophesied about you hypocrites; as it is written: 'These people honor me with their lips, but their hearts are far from me. They worship me in vain; their teachings are merely human rules.' You have let go of the commands of God and are holding on to human traditions."
—Mark 7:6–8

Politics as well as Religion has its superstitions. These, gaining strength with time, may, one day, give imaginary value to this relic, for its association with the birth of the Great Charter of our Independence.
—Thomas Jefferson, letter to Joseph Coolidge Jr. Nov. 18, 1825, commenting on his portable writing desk used for writing the Declaration of Independence

One of the values of a movement like Friends is our long history. One of the dangers of a movement like Friends is our long history.

Our history works for us when we tap into our values and precepts that informed the movement in the first place. The immediacy of Christ, the presence of the Holy Spirit in each believer, the urgency of proclamation, and the equality of all in Christ provide a few examples.

On the other hand, our history works against us when we codify practices of minor significance. (Remember "Quaker gray?") Or when we hang on too long to practices that had a meaningful role at one point but later become obstacles to communicating the gospel (like plain speech).

When I read the above comment by Jefferson, it reminded me of Jesus' rebuke quoted in Mark. We do have a natural bent toward the collection of relics and traditions. When a Pharisee or a church or a movement gives into this bent, however, it exacts a high cost on our witness.

To all of us inclined to cling to "human traditions," Jesus said, you "nullify the word of God by your tradition that you have handed down" (Mark 7:13). Ouch. Do any of us really want those words on our tombstone?

As leaders, as followers of Jesus, we have a responsibility to continually evaluate our lives and ministries in the light of Scripture.

Am I keeping the main thing the main thing? Am I more in love with the gift wrapping than the Gift?

Risk and Rest

Abide in me and I in you. As the branch cannot bear
fruit by itself, unless it abides in the vine, neither can
you, unless you abide in me.

—John 15:4 (ESV)

At a time of confusion and pain in my personal life, I
stumbled onto John 15. I was relatively new to life in
Christ and had just entered into my first major crisis
of faith. I felt cornered by circumstances and wondered where God was. Then I read John 15 and understood: God was with me in the furnace inviting me
to abide—to rest—in the divine Presence. It helped
a bit to learn this, but I confess the "divine solution"
appeared heavy with personal risk.

Day by day I would reread John 15, and slowly,
across the days of my isolation, the reality of God's
presence and the sufficiency of God's plan for me
relaxed my soul. I began to find peace and rest in a
situation that was tumultuous and threatening.

I vividly remember the day I ceased striving and
chose to rest instead. I released myself and my future
into God's hands and actually rejoiced in the decision

to do so. My relationship with God entered into a new, still clumsy season of growth.

Yes, it was unsettling to relinquish control and embrace the risk of the unknown, but I felt confident in the One to whom I surrendered. I *knew* God would treat me well. Not the way I desired, perhaps, but well all the same.

I do not think I have ever looked back from that moment. However imperfectly I may have done so, I have staked everything on Jesus. I have occasionally come to crossroads where the best option seemed terrifyingly "risky," but knowing the One who called me forward made all the difference.

Perhaps the greatest risk is to resist God's call on our lives.

Do I hear the invitation from Jesus to abide in him as a risk or as a rest from my striving?

Corinth Is Everywhere

Every day they continued to meet together in the
temple courts. They broke bread in their homes and ate
together with glad and sincere hearts, praising God and
enjoying the favor of all the people. And the Lord added
to their number daily those who were being saved.
—Acts 2:46–47

I appeal to you, brothers and sisters, in the name of
our Lord Jesus Christ, that all of you agree with one
another in what you say and that there be no divisions
among you, but that you be perfectly united in mind
and thought. My brothers and sisters, some from
Chloe's household have informed me that there are
quarrels among you.
—1 Corinthians 1:10–11

A friend and I were discussing evangelism,
discipleship, and the challenges of sharing the gospel
in a globalized world. We agreed that one of the
impediments to discipling has to do with the lack of
a common culture.

As we assembled a list of the obstacles globaliza-
tion creates, I blurted out, "It's because in the twenty-
first century, Corinth is everywhere!" He looked at

me quizzically, so I explained: "Jerusalem was mono-cultural, but when Paul entered Europe, especially Corinth, he found himself in a radically different context. The strategies the disciples used in Jerusalem were useless—for example, there was no temple for gathering and preaching, and there was no common cultural narrative."

When we look at the church in Jerusalem, we find a population that was Jewish except for the Roman soldiers. For the disciples, the temple provided a great fishing hole, and they had a plethora of shared stories, convictions, and experiences with the rest of the city's population.

The entire city of Jerusalem was at least aware of Jesus, so evangelism had a much more developed starting point. In addition, there were recognized ways to disciple that everyone understood. Oh, and they all liked the same casseroles.

Then there was Corinth. Fractious, perverse, brawling Corinth of a hundred ethnic groups and languages shaken together in a seaport. (Think: bar scene in *Star Wars: Episode IV*.) The Scriptures and the good news of Jesus? Completely unknown.

Yes, believers fought in Jerusalem as well as in Corinth, but in Jerusalem they were family feuds; everyone knew the rules. In Corinth the fights were over new issues—shocking at times for an ex-Pharisee like Paul—and new rules were constantly being created because, well, there were no rules. Paul had no game book to follow; he had to write it. Several times.

Today, as far as the church is concerned, everywhere is Corinth. In the past the church in America enjoyed seasons of at least regional cultural homogeneity (probably more imagined than real), but those days are over. So what do we do? We can lament the lost past or we can imitate Paul: plunge in, assess what works and what doesn't, adjust, and repeat.

Paul's approach assumed a messy process, expected occasional grief, and trusted God would break in and do something awesome. Paul's methodology allowed the gospel to expand out of the Jewish ghettos across the Roman Empire and penetrate whole cities.

I'm sure the Corinthians aged Paul prematurely, but with all the grief they caused him as they learned how to follow Jesus, he could still say, "I take great pride in you. I am greatly encouraged; in all our troubles my joy knows no bounds" (2 Corinthians 7:4).

Everywhere is Corinth—including where we live. What are we, as a local church, going to do about it?

Even Him?

The saying is trustworthy and deserving of full
acceptance, that Christ Jesus came into the world to
save sinners, of whom I am the foremost.
—1 Timothy 1:15 (ESV)

And when Ahab heard those words, he tore his clothes
and put sackcloth on his flesh and fasted and lay in
sackcloth and went about dejectedly. And the word of
the LORD came to Elijah the Tishbite, saying, "Have
you seen how Ahab has humbled himself before me?
Because he has humbled himself . . . I will not bring the
disaster in his days."
—1 Kings 21:27–29a (ESV)

I am surprised Shakespeare never wrote a play about
Ahab. His life includes all the elements we normal-
ly associate with a great theatrical tragedy: hunger
for power, a manipulative spouse, a tortured will, a
double-minded soul. One finds him at turns vile and
pathetic, arrogant and laughable, and completely cast
about by events.

Scripture makes clear Ahab was no innocent;
essentially he sold his soul to evil. Again and again

when confronted with God's power or God's grace, he refused to change.

And yet.

This king who bears more responsibility than almost any other for the spiritual bankruptcy of Israel is also the only king in Israel's shameful history who publicly repented. And God heard him! Yes, Ahab still ended badly because he was unable to discern between godly counsel and the sycophants surrounding him. Nonetheless, he experienced some measure of God's grace when we would have expected God to respond with scorn.

Why would God waste love and mercy on a wretch like Ahab? Because the same God who declares, "You shall be holy to me, for I the LORD am holy" (Leviticus 20:26 ESV), also tells us, "I have no pleasure in the death of anyone" (Ezekiel 18:32 ESV).

I confess I do not truly comprehend divine love extended to a king like Ahab—or to, say, a human trafficker. Yet Ahab's experience underlines what Paul, "the worst of all sinners," tried to explain to Timothy: God loves us with incomprehensible grace—amazing grace. It extends to slave traders like John Newton, idolaters like Ahab, and cowards like me.

As Paul concludes, "But I received mercy for this reason, that in me, as the foremost, Jesus Christ might display his perfect patience as an example to those who were to believe in him for eternal life" (1 Timothy 1:16 ESV).

Is there anyone in my circle of relationships that I have given up on? How would God have me pray for them and continue reaching out?

Our Matchless Inheritance

Be careful to follow all the commands of the Lord your God, that you may possess this good land and pass it on as an inheritance to your descendants forever. And you, my son Solomon, acknowledge the God of your father, and serve him with wholehearted devotion and with a willing mind, for the Lord searches every heart and understands every desire and every thought. If you seek him, he will be found by you; but if you forsake him, he will reject you forever.

—1 Chronicles 28:8b–9

I met up with a friend who told me he had just brought his family together with a trusted financial advisor. The purpose of the meeting? To talk about the future: financial planning, God's purposes for their family and the resources they manage, and the values that inform the way they steward, spend, and invest God's wealth.

He wanted his children to know what they would need to do to grow God's assets and provide a kingdom impact and financial legacy for their children's children. I was impressed.

The following morning I read the passage quoted above. It struck me that my friend (unknowingly, perhaps) had done exactly what David had done with his son Solomon and the people of Israel, as recounted in 1 Chronicles. Both my friend and King David understood that inheritances are gifts—whether the inheritance is economic, spiritual, relational, or otherwise. Inheritances come to us apart from anything we have done. However, the only reason inheritances exist is because the ones who give to us have made careful provisions for the gifts. We inherit from our parents because they intentionally developed and preserved the inheritance for us.

As followers of Jesus, we inherit eternal life because God intentionally provided a Redeemer for us in a plan that was made before the foundation of the world (Ephesians 1). This inheritance, far beyond any inheritance given from parents to children, is the defining expression of God's incomprehensible love for us.

Am I walking in the joy and bounty of this inheritance? Has its breadth and length and height and depth (Ephesians 3:18) captured my soul and imagination?

Hate

> I have a message from God in my heart
> concerning the sinfulness of the wicked:
> There is no fear of Go before their eyes.
> In their own eyes they flatter themselves
> too much to detect or hate their sin.
> The words of their mouths
> are wicked and deceitful;
> they fail to act wisely or do good.
> Even on their beds they plot evil;
> they commit themselves to a sinful course
> and do not reject what is wrong.
> —Psalm 36:1–4

Emmanuel. God with us.

What happened at Emmanuel African Episcopal Church when a young white man entered a prayer meeting and slaughtered the African American worshipers has received commentary from far weightier folk than yours truly. The most eloquent and powerful words came from the mouths of those directly impacted.

Saints indeed. Many of the surviving victims as well as family members of the martyrs found strength and will to extend love and forgiveness to the perpetrator. To do this so quickly after the murders reflects a spirituality for which I can only aim.

I wish I could say I do not understand the perpetrator. I wish I could dismiss him as subhuman. Sadly, however, he is perfectly human. Or at least he is frighteningly like me.

When I read about injustices in other places or merely have to deal with someone who thinks my lawn and their dog belong together, my private thoughts can go to frightful, retributive places with alarming speed. By God's grace I also have the Holy Spirit's brakes. Appropriately rebuked (and convicted), I turn to prayer for my suffering brethren and their persecutors or get the shovel and move on with my life.

But what if I did not have the Spirit's restraint? What if I did not have a heart in a process of transformation? What would constrain my bent toward evil? "The heart is deceitful above all things and beyond cure. Who can understand it?" (Jeremiah 17:9).

Sadly, Lord, I can understand it. But praise God for God's grace, for the work of Jesus Christ, and for the work of the Holy Spirit that cleanses even the hardest heart.

The psalmist's words after the passage quoted at the beginning of this reflection juxtapose the heart of the wicked with the love of God: "Your love, Lord,

reaches to the heavens, your faithfulness to the skies. .
. . How priceless is your unfailing love, O God! *People
take refuge in the shadow of your wings*" (Psalm 36:5, 7,
emphasis mine).

In Emmanuel we find refuge. And Life. And
power over hate.

Let's go tell it. Let's live it.

*In what direct fashion would God have me contribute to
the ongoing healing of our nation's wounds?*

Who Am I Really?

> David asked, "Is there anyone still left of the house of
> Saul to whom I can show kindness
> for Jonathan's sake?"
> —2 Samuel 9:1

Years ago I shared a book with a friend. It was *Leap
Over a Wall* by Eugene Peterson, a study of the life of
King David. In a recent letter my friend referred to a
particular chapter in which Peterson explored David's
relationship with Mephibosheth. Mephibosheth was
the son of David's best friend, Jonathan.

After Jonathan and his father, King Saul, died in
battle, a nurse fled with the child Mephibosheth. In
her haste to escape, she dropped him, and he became
crippled as a result (2 Samuel 4:4). He had lived
anonymously—and probably with no small amount
of fear—ever since. Three thousand years ago, common practice when one ruling house supplanted
another included exterminating the "competition;"
Mephibosheth and his protectors would have known
this. In adulthood he would have been unable to
work, and as a member of the deposed royal family, he

was a potential liability to anyone who housed him. We might call him "toxic waste."

David, however, seeks him out to bless him in memory of Jonathan. David provides Mephibosheth with a seat at the king's table; he commands Saul's former servant and his family to permanently serve Mephibosheth and his son. The Scriptures tell us Mephibosheth sat at the table "like one of the king's sons" (2 Samuel 9:11).

An amazing story of grace to be sure. This was my friend's comment to me: "I realized . . . I am Mephibosheth, bound by limitation, damaged by misinformed beliefs, held captive by the twisted expectations of this world's upside-down culture . . . but invited, freed, and brought to his table by my Savior, Jesus Christ!"

I loved his assessment. Indeed, we are *all* Mephibosheths. My friend had provided me with both a beautiful insight and an instructive caution. It is easy to sit at the King's table and forget I have crippled feet, while judging the deformities of others.

Sometimes my judgmental eye turns toward those within the house of faith. Sure, we have a responsibility to hold one another accountable, to call sin what it is, and occasionally to call one another to repentance—but they should be conversations fueled by love and our ministry of reconciliation

(2 Corinthians 5:19). When I forget this and operate out of mixed motives, God is not glorified.

There are other times when my judgmental eye turns outside the church and focuses upon persecutors, critics, mockers, or those who are merely weak. I sit at the table and shake my head with loathing at the cripples outside the door, unmindful of my own clubbed feet swinging busily under my seat. I forget I sit at the table only because Jesus sat me there.

Lord, guard me from the sin of pride—help me extend to others the same mercy you show to me.

Who are the Mephibosheths in my life at this moment? To whom can I extend the generous grace and forgiveness of God—and a seat at the table?

Redemption

Zion will be delivered with justice,
her penitent ones with righteousness.
—Isaiah 1:27

Fear not, for I have redeemed you.
—Isaiah 43:1 (NKJV)

The book of Isaiah does not begin with good news. God declares Israel is dumber than a donkey (1:3), rotten to the core (1:4), stubborn to the point of self-destruction (1:5–6), and all but destroyed (1:7).

The prophetic word only grows fiercer as God continues cataloging their collective sin and pending punishment. Yet one tiny glimmer of hope appears just before Isaiah's first pronouncement concludes. Verse 27 speaks of Zion's redemption.

Notice the use of the passive tense: "Zion will be delivered with justice"—not "Zion shall redeem herself." Whatever is going to happen to redeem God's people, the redemption will come from outside. Isaiah 42:6 tells us whose righteousness will redeem Israel (and the other nations): the Messiah's.

Beginning with chapter 43, the words *redeem* and *redeemer* repeatedly punctuate the text. God unfolds the divine plan of redemption, of rescue. God relentlessly drives home the point: God has redeemed us; God has paid the price. The Messiah becomes our substitute when he "makes his life an offering for sin" (53:10b).

Glory!

On several recent occasions, I have heard Christians ask why God did not redeem us another way. Why did God not simply declare us forgiven? The question indicates either an embarrassingly low view of sin and its consequences or an inflated view of self. God does what must be done to extend grace and uphold the law by paying the price in our stead.

The next time you read Isaiah, pay attention to how often God adds *redeemer* to his identity (43:1; 43:14; 44:6; 44:22, 24; etc.). God takes our relationship out of the realm of transaction and brings it into the realm of self-giving, self-sacrificing love established on a foundation of divine holiness.

> And can it be that I should gain
> An interest in the Savior's blood
> Died He for me, who caused His pain—
> For me who Him to death pursued?
> (Charles Wesley)

When did I last pause and reflect on the magnitude of God's unfathomable gift?

When Societies Collapse

Thus you are to say to him, "Thus says the LORD, 'Behold, what I have built I am about to tear down, and what I have planted I am about to uproot, that is, the whole land. But you, are you seeking great things for yourself? Do not seek them; for behold, I am going to bring disaster on all flesh,' declares the LORD, 'but I will give your life to you as booty in all the places where you may go.'"

—Jeremiah 45:4–5 (NASB 1995)

I read Jeremiah's prophecies against Israel's neighbors, having just finished David Abulafia's history of the Mediterranean, *The Great Sea*. I was struck by an interesting connection. Abulafia traces the rise and decline of scores of civilizations and empires; Jeremiah records the conversation between God and a handful of those same nations—among others, Israel and Judah, Philistia, and Egypt.

The prophecies ring terrifying in their severity and thoroughness. The finality explicit in the declarations—there is no "lifeline" option—left me wondering how a disciple of Jesus living here in the US might manage living faithfully in a time of social collapse or divine judgment.

Whether one believes the US is on a downward spiral toward apocalypse or plunging like the phoenix into fire and rebirth or merely wandering aimlessly without a meaningful vision, there seems to be a general sense of angst about what's coming next. Jeremiah's generation certainly could relate: threatened alternately by Assyria, Babylon, and Egypt, repeatedly betrayed by their neighbors, people were anxious. Jeremiah's unwelcomed prophetic ministry fueled fear and infuriated kings.

In the midst of the kingdom's freefall, a couple of individuals stood out: Ebedmelech, an Ethiopian eunuch in the king's house (see ch. 38 and 39:16–18), and Baruch, Jeremiah's scribe (ch. 45). Both chose to align their lives with God and the prophet Jeremiah, living at odds with everyone else in Jerusalem. What did their faithfulness look like?

They did not display their devotion to God from a rooftop, but they elected to consistently do the right thing whenever they had an opportunity. They determined to live quiet, fearless lives of obedience to God and service to their neighbors. Humble steadfastness characterized their walk and serves as an example for our own.

What might such a life look like today? Who is the Jeremiah in my life in desperate need of a companion?

Of Ministry and Loss

The word of the LORD came to me: "Son of man,
with one blow I am about to take away from you the
delight of your eyes. Yet do not lament or weep or shed
any tears. Groan quietly; do not mourn for the dead.
Keep your turban fastened and your sandals on your
feet; do not cover the lower part of your face or eat
the customary food [of mourners]." So I spoke to the
people in the morning, and in the evening my wife died.
The next morning I did as I had been commanded.
—Ezekiel 24:15-18

For anyone who has a transactional view of faith,
this passage is potentially devastating. Ezekiel had
witnessed visions of God. Ezekiel had done *everything*
God had required of him. Ezekiel had suffered
persistently in the exercise of his prophetic ministry.
Now this.

If Ezekiel wasn't safe from suffering, who is?

Transactional faith has no boxes for a passage
like this one. Instead it declares, "If I do what God
asks, God must take care of me," or as Satan said to
Jesus, "For it is written: 'He will command his angels

concerning you . . . so that you will not strike your foot against a stone'" (Matthew 4:6).

I fully agree that the life of a disciple will generally prove much more satisfying than the life of one who ignores God—but painless? Free from loss? No.

Dietrich Bonhoeffer said, "When Christ calls a man, He bids him 'come and die.'" In my observation, obedience has carried with it betrayal, periodic isolation, character assassination, and unfathomable loss (personal loved ones or trusted coworkers).

If this is the case, why does anyone stick it out? How in the world did Ezekiel keep his faith when told his ministry would now include losing "the delight of [his] eyes"? My first response is to say, "I have no idea," but that is not true. I do know. Ezekiel had seen visions of God. Ezekiel had a calling from God. Ezekiel knew how the story would end (see ch. 40-48). As wretched as his circumstances became, he knew God was ultimately faithful . . . and worth the suffering.

What about me? What do I think God "owes" me because I have responded to the call? Am I willing to follow Jesus no matter the cost? Can I truly say with Job, "Though he slay me, yet will I hope in him"? (Job 13:15)

Listen to Him

There [Jesus] was transfigured before them. His face
shone like the sun, and his clothes became as white as
the light. Just then there appeared before them Moses
and Elijah, talking with Jesus. Peter said to Jesus, "Lord,
it is good for us to be here. If you wish, I will put up
three shelters—one for you, one for Moses and one
for Elijah." While he was still speaking, a bright cloud
covered them, and a voice from the cloud said, "This
is my Son, whom I love; with him I am well pleased.
Listen to him!"
—Matthew 17:2-5

A week prior to this account, Jesus had told his disciples the cost of following him: self-denial—death
to self. And then? "Follow me" (Matthew 16:24).
Now we find him leading three of them up on a
mountaintop.

What follows rocks their world. The carpenter,
their rabbi, reveals his divine self to them. To make
the moment even more dramatic, Moses and Elijah
appear and converse with him. It is one of those
sublime moments that begs for reverent silence and
worship.

Instead, Peter starts talking. (He must be my ancestor!)

Have you ever found yourself talking, when suddenly you became painfully conscious how inappropriate you sounded—and simultaneously aware how impotent you were to stop babbling? Peter does this, and God mercifully speaks over Peter's chatter.

In his defense, Peter did recognize the majesty of the moment and wanted to do *something* in response. However, his solution reveals how little he had understood: "Let's build three booths." Peter thought he was dealing with three equals. God stopped this notion with a clear command: "Listen to him."

Commentators generally agree that Moses and Elijah represent the Law and the Prophets. Jesus stands among these two symbols of the Scriptures as the one who fulfills their words. In fact, he is the one who *supplants* them. Their time has passed; Jesus now replaces the tutelage of the Old Testament with a relationship (Galatians 3:24). God instructs Peter, "This is my Son. . . . Listen to him!"

For years I would read this sentence as, "*Listen* to him." However, at some point it struck me God probably said, "Listen to *him*" (not to the Law and the Prophets). Moses and Elijah have done their work, and the written Word now is to be interpreted in the light of the living Word.

Why the change in the way I read the emphasis? Because in verse 8, Matthew tells us, "When they looked up, they saw no one except Jesus." No Moses. No Elijah. No tabernacle. No altars. Just Jesus.

Listen to *him*.

Whose voice fills my ears and has the greatest influence on my life and ministry?

Who Moved Our Church?

> When you come to appear before me, who has asked
> this of you, this trampling of my courts? Stop bringing
> meaningless offerings! Your incense is detestable to me.
> New Moons, Sabbaths and convocations—I cannot
> bear your evil assemblies. Your New Moon festivals and
> your appointed feasts my soul hates. They have become
> a burden to me; I am weary of bearing them.
> —Isaiah 1:12-14

It must have staggered Jerusalem to hear these words from God. For about 350 years, the temple had served as the focus of God's worship, and now God was telling them, "This is *your* religion, not *mine*."

Listeners must have wondered, "When did things change? When did our temple 'change hands' in God's mind and cease being the site of Yahweh's worship? What should we do now?"

The American church has experienced a similar dislocation; however, in our case the rejection has come from our culture rather than God. Over the past fifty years, popular culture has slowly and inexorably pushed the church from the center of culture to the very margin—and even beyond.

Seemingly, we went to bed one night as the "Great Culture Arbitrator" and woke up the next morning plopped outside the city gates. Unfortunately, some Christians continue to behave as if nothing has changed—they don't understand why no one pays attention to them, and they demand an audience. Others recognize the change and loudly protest, "Who moved our church?!"

The situation presents us with a few options: (1) ignore the new reality, (2) protest the new reality and demand we be let back in (you decide if this has possibilities), or (3) accept the new paradigm and adapt to a new strategy. In this last scenario, the church adopts a missionary posture and reengages culture as the bringer of good news.

If we opt for the last strategy and view ourselves as missionaries, we will necessarily cast aside our ascribed status and adopt a *new* status: learners. In our role as learners, we will prioritize listening and observing. Later, armed with new understanding, we can become servants. Out of our servant's posture, we will engage the culture as ones who *esteem* the insiders—rather than resenting them. As we serve we will eventually become friends. Out of this new relationship, doors periodically open to tell God's story.

Learner, servant, friend, storyteller—this is one method for engaging culture when somebody moves your church.

How comfortable am I with the concept of my church as a missional community on the periphery of culture? What would it look like for me to adapt to the new reality?

The Leadership Coin

I hope in the Lord Jesus to send Timothy to you
soon. . . . I have no one else like him.
—Philippians 2:19–20

The buck stops here.
—President Harry Truman

There is no limit to the amount of good you can do if
you don't care who gets the credit.
—President Ronald Reagan

I recently read an article about a seventy-four-year-old retired college football coach who took over a disastrously bad high school team near his home. This team had *never* had a winning season and had not won a game in the previous three years.

Coach Uzelac took them to the playoffs that year (2015), and along the way, his example galvanized city businesses, churches, and the high school itself around a new vision for the team. A number of other people have subsequently stepped up and made significant contributions of their own.

Two quotes popped into my mind as I read the article: Harry Truman's famous line about the presidency and Ronald Reagan's philosophy of leadership. At the same moment, it also occurred to me that Truman and Reagan were expressing the two sides of the "effective leadership" coin: taking full responsibility for outcomes while offering full-empowerment that celebrates success in others.

Charles H. Townes modeled the same philosophy in science. Townes is considered the inventor of the laser. He left a legacy of mentoring and empowering those coming behind him; my guess is that at least ten of his protégés received Nobel prizes. In fact, whether we talk about football, science, politics, the church, or any other context, these two principles apply.

One reason for Paul's prominence in early church history is the emphasis he placed on disciple-making. He took responsibility for the ministry started in each city but quickly identified local leaders whom he could equip. He would then assign a couple of the key developing leaders on his team to work with and continue training the emerging leaders of the new church. His protégés were charged with discipling and training the growing congregation.

Paul took care to honor those whom he equipped—his comments about Timothy quoted above are similar to the praise he expressed for Mark, Titus, Apollo, Tychicus, Epaphroditus, Phoebe, and a host of others. Who received the respect? They did. Paul was okay with this—and it led to a host of new ministers with similar convictions about equipping and celebrating others.

What about me? Do I own the failures and shortfalls in my ministry or blame others? Do I set others up to succeed in their calling and celebrate them when they do? Whom have I praised publicly the way Paul praised Timothy?

Rest

Then the Lord said to Moses, "How long will you refuse
to keep my commands and my instructions? Bear in
mind that the Lord has given you the Sabbath; that is
why on the sixth day he gives you bread for two days.
Everyone is to stay where they are on the seventh day;
no one is to go out."
—Exodus 16:28–29a, 30

Leaders are tempted to give 115 percent, to "leave it
all on the field," because giving beyond expectations
is viewed as noble. But leaders don't live on the field,
they live at home. If they leave it all on the field, they go
home with nothing.
—Albert Tate

God has included an important insight for us in the
book of Exodus. At the time God provided manna
for the people of Israel, God also made provision
for them to preserve the Sabbath rest by collecting a
double portion on the sixth day. Why does it matter?

The conversation between Moses and God
recorded in chapter 16 occurred before God's meeting with Moses on Mount Sinai. In other words,

before Moses descended the mountain with the Ten Commandments in chapter 20, God had reestablished the Sabbath rest as an integral part of Israel's identity.

This reestablishment of the Sabbath rest after years of slavery in Egypt was not based on the law; rather, it was evidently based on the Creation event (Genesis 2:2–3). With this in mind, we have no reason to write off the importance of Sabbath rest for our own lives.

Jesus, when accused of ignoring the Sabbath, did not dismiss it in his response. Instead Jesus told his listeners, "The Sabbath was made for man, not man for the Sabbath" (Mark 2:27). Jesus upheld the value of rest but returned it to its proper role as a blessing for us.

The modern world has made a virtue of "leaving it all on the field"—we celebrate athletes who never miss a game, or the CEO who loses health and family for the company. But this kind of "sacrifice" does not please God.

Pastors and other ministers are not immune to the same misconception. Because the stakes are so high—individual transformation, the salvation of the world—internal guilt asks us how one can rest when people's eternal destinies are on the line. Therefore, many among us skip days off and work long hours to "take care of business." It sounds noble; however, it can sometimes disguise the *real* thought: "Nobody can do this like I can; God needs me."

The instructions God gave to Israel in the desert suggest God does not see life and ministry this way.

The Sabbath did at least three things for Israel: First, it reminded them of their dependence upon their Creator for life. Second, it reminded them their daily provision came from God—a demonstration of God's goodness. Finally, setting aside a day each week to worship, and to enjoy creation, family, and community, also protected them (along with their servants and farm animals) from overworking.

No, we are not bound to the Mosaic Sabbath as found in the law; however, regular periodic rest is a gift from God to keep us balanced and renewed. Receive it.

Am I afraid of rest? Do I work hard and maintain healthy boundaries?

Leading with Open Hands

The Lord said to Moses, "Go up into this mountain of Abarim and see the land that I have given to the people of Israel. When you have seen it, you also shall be gathered to your people." . . . Moses spoke to the Lord, saying, "Let the Lord, the God of the spirits of all flesh, appoint a man over the congregation." . . . So the Lord said to Moses, "Take Joshua the son of Nun, a man in whom is the Spirit."
—Numbers 27:12–13a, 15–16, 18a (ESV)

Moses herded cats for forty years. Mean, complaining, rebellious, unteachable cats. (Dog lovers will ask me, "Is there any other kind of cat?!")

He led them with open hands. When the weight of leadership overwhelmed him, he did not cling to a position; rather, he invited God to remove him (ch. 11). God responded by giving Moses seventy Spirit-filled elders so he would not "bear it yourself alone" (11:17 ESV).

When Moses' older brother and sister—his coleaders—wanted to replace him, he did not get defensive. He let God choose who would lead Israel (ch. 12). Moses also interceded on behalf of Aaron and Miriam when God punished them for their rebellion.

Later, the people of Israel rejected God's instructions to enter the promised land and wanted to stone Moses (ch. 14). God considered pouring divine wrath on them, but Moses interceded on their behalf.

You get the idea.

Moses practiced leading with open hands, willing to lead as long as God required it of him but not clinging to power or position.

I think Moses' most impressive example of open-handed leadership occurs in chapter 27 of Numbers. God had announced to Moses that his tenure as Israel's leader was over. Moses was going to die. Moses responded by pleading for a new leader who " shall lead them out and bring them in" (Numbers 27:17 ESV).

Notice, Moses did not propose his sons. He did not propose Aaron's sons. He did not even propose Joshua, whom he had discipled for forty years. He simply asked for a gracious leader and put the role and the responsibility in God's hands—where they belonged.

And when God chose Joshua? "Moses *did as the Lord commanded him*. He took Joshua and made him stand before Eleazar the priest and the whole congregation, and he laid his hands on him and

commissioned him as the Lord directed" (Numbers
27:22–23 ESV, emphasis mine).

Do I hold my ministry with open hands? How regularly do I intercede for those who oppose my leadership or attack my person? How willingly would I hand over the reins?

Following

Then they answered Joshua, "Whatever you have
commanded us we will do, and wherever you send us
we will go. Just as we fully obeyed Moses, so we will
obey you."
—Joshua 1:16–17a

In the last reflection, we looked at leadership as
modeled by Moses and ended with his replacement
by Joshua. When one begins reading in Joshua, one
cannot help being struck by the above passage—it
invites us to reflect on the other half of leadership:
following.

Here's the point: the people talking to Joshua in
these verses are the children of the men and wom-
en who made life *impossible* for Moses. "Just as we
obeyed Moses in all things. . . ." Their parents could
never have uttered those words. The older generation
complained about the lack of water and complained
about the lack of food. When God provided food,
they complained about that too ("No more mana!").
They repeatedly challenged Moses' leadership and
regularly questioned his decisions.

Apparently, the children learned something from the outcome of their parents' rebelliousness. Remember, God told the Israelites than no one over the age of twenty would enter the promised land since they had doubted God's ability to give it to them. As the children grew into adulthood, it seems they chose to listen to Moses—most of the time, at least. Now in the handoff, they publicly transfer their allegiance to Joshua.

This is my takeaway: if godly leadership is open-handed, so is godly followership. When our local church or our own ministry team makes a decision, we may not get our way; but this is where we trust God with the results of decisions made by prayer and wise counsel.

And we don't walk out just because we don't like the decision. We determine to stay engaged, stay committed, and pray for our team or church. By staying involved—with open hands—we keep ourselves open to new things God may want to do with us or through us, things we might miss if we choose to leave.

Are those who watch my lead learning how to follow with open hands?

Do I trust God to lead through others?

The Cost of Leadership

As for you, always be sober-minded, endure suffering,
do the work of an evangelist, fulfill your ministry.
—2 Timothy 4:5 (ESV)

A friend of mine formerly ministered in a semiclosed country and even planted a church there. One day he told me the church he helped plant had been closed down by the authorities.

The church became a victim of its own success—too many people responded to the gospel. The congregation jettisoned their invisibility—with the relative safety that went with it—and consequently became a target of the police.

"What will they do now?" I asked. He responded by showing me a photo he had received. The church's small group leaders were being prayed over and commissioned as pastors of their new little churches. This was their response. The decision to shut down one church resulted in the birth of twenty new ones!

Opposition and persecution are trademarks of church life in my friend's country. When their

95

churches have camps or retreats, they often include a special service with an invitation to ministry. As a part of the invitation, campers are reminded that pastoral ministry means being the last to leave when a church is raided—in order to insure the brethren escape. It also means assuming you will be jailed—or worse.

He told me brothers and sisters *always* come forward at these services despite the warnings regarding the high price of the pastoral call. Pastoring, as Christians in his country understand it, means doing time in prison.

What price am I willing to pay for the privilege of serving God?

Taking Counsel

> When he saw Elijah, he said to him, "Is that you, you
> troubler of Israel?"
> —1 Kings 18:17

When we launched our ministry, I had the opportunity to meet periodically with some church planters and a couple of coaches. Although each of us worked independently, we met to examine some aspect of planting together and to critique one another's efforts.

The process helped me immensely. Having good coaching protected me from fixating on only one aspect of ministry development and forgetting the rest. The others kept me moving and attentive to the details that would matter more as the ministry grew.

One week we looked at our disciple-making process and were asked to make a visual illustration of the process. Well, perhaps you have heard Proverbs 27:6: "Faithful are the wounds of a friend; profuse are the kisses of an enemy" (ESV).

It came to mind when I considered how our meeting had gone. Whereas I thought my illustration was crystal clear, my friends and coaches all thought it was clear as mud. Their comments were not intended to insult me at all; they wanted to help me become more effective. They gave me good counsel to clean it up. However, I had wanted praise—not more work! Nevertheless, I returned home and did as instructed.

God put Elijah in King Ahab's life to turn him and his kingdom back to God. Sadly, Ahab regarded Elijah as a meddler and source of inconvenient truths. Ahab's unwillingness to listen ultimately cost him his life; it would cost his descendants the kingdom.

That is the way godly counsel works. Someone who loves us and wants the best for us calls us to acknowledge a place of brokenness or failure. If we receive the counsel and apply it, the changes can take us to a new level of fruitfulness or spiritual growth.

On the other hand, we can ignore counsel given in love and embrace stubbornness (or rebellion) instead. Ahab's end serves as a warning to those unwilling to listen. Proverbs has something to say about that option as well: "There is a way which seems right to a person, But its end is the way of death" (Proverbs 14:12 NASB).

To what degree have I demonstrated a teachable heart to those who love me and seek to help me avoid self-inflicted pain or failure?

Hard Heads, Hard Hearts, High Hope

> Zedekiah was twenty-one years old when he became
> king. . . . He did evil in the eyes of the Lord, just as
> Jehoiakim had done.
> —2 Kings 24:18a, 19

During an election year, a friend sent me a Peggy Noonan article. In it Noonan lamented the loss of civility and integrity in the public space, illustrated by the candidates for national office.

At the time I had been reading 2 Kings. It is a heartbreaking read and one that always stymies my imagination. What prompted Manasseh to become the spiritual and ethical antithesis of his father Hezekiah? Why did Josiah's sons consistently choose political suicide despite divine warnings? How could the people of Israel and Judah so quickly turn from God to worshipping Baal, Molech, Astarte, and other junior-grade divinities?

Then I look at our own social milieu or read an article like Noonan's, and I understand: spiritual collapse can arrive in a moment. For a variety of reasons, devotion to God simply ceases to inspire; instead the gods of sex and sensuality—whether called Baal or Prince—capture the collective imagination.

Reading 2 Kings while simultaneously watching our society in the midst of a meltdown of meaning, I find I have greater appreciation for Israel's rapid decline. The Jewish people simply lost faith: faith in God, faith in the value of godliness, faith in their identity as God's people.

They opted instead for a belief system in which everyone was out for their own good. Baal and friends played perfectly to such a world view: they pandered to the lusts and desires of their devotees and required nothing beyond the occasional sacrifice (including child sacrifice). Without a moral framework, the social fabric quickly unraveled, and prophetic warnings could not sway a nation bent on self-gratification.

We seem to find ourselves in a similar circumstance—with one difference. We can offer more than warnings of doom. We do not have to resign ourselves to lament, like Jeremiah or Noonan. By God's grace we have the message of God's kingdom, the power of God's Spirit in us, and our "blessed hope" (Titus 2:13).

How can I most effectively be good news in such times?

Does the church have a responsibility to model a different hope? If so, what does it look like?

The Holy, Joyful God

> And God saw everything that he had made, and behold,
> it was very good.
> —Genesis 1:31a (ESV)

> This is a God bathed world.
> —Dallas Willard, *The Divine Conspiracy*

If you ever have the opportunity, I hope you visit the Toledo Cathedral in Spain, what I call "the church of the exuberant angels." In a dome *filled* with light, angel statues play, tumble, summersault, and party in the presence of God. I have never seen anything like it anywhere. The artists knew something about God that much of medieval Spain had forgotten: God rejoices.

One Sunday in a ministry session, we discussed Dallas Willard's reflections on the immanence and transcendence of God. After establishing how utterly perfect and complete and outside of creation God is, Willard then turns to God's total engagement with creation and the great joy—the giddiness (my word, not Willard's)—suffusing the Creator's contemplation of his handiwork.

God is not a "morose monarch, a frustrated and petty parent," observes Willard; no, God is Author of the universe, our Creator, our Pursuer, and he takes great joy in creation. After all, how dour can the author of the platypus be?

This is a side of God we tend to forget in our preoccupation with our sinful, marauding human selves. Yet God has created a universe saturated with incomprehensible beauty and, in Jesus, taken up redemptive residence within one broken tidbit of the glorious whole—our planet. Unfathomable.

And then, even more incomprehensibly, God names us, telling us, "You are mine" (Isaiah 43:1).

Yes, according to Psalm 139, the same One who spun stars and galaxies into existence also knit me in my mother's womb. And you in yours. The same can be said for every other person on this planet. I believe God has made these truths known to us in order to radically alter the way we walk in this world and perceive our neighbors.

Later that same afternoon, I asked the interns in the ministry session a question: Tell about a time when you *knew* you were in the presence of our joy-filled God, swept away by the overwhelming power of God's presence and God's love and holiness and goodness. What did you learn?

How might I answer that question?

Leading through Law or Grace

They entered into a covenant to seek the Lord, the God
of their ancestors, with all their heart and soul. All who
would not seek the Lord, the God of Israel, were to be
put to death, whether small or great,
man or woman.
—2 Chronicles 15:12–13

Jehoshaphat lived in Jerusalem, and he went out again
among the people from Beersheba to the hill country of
Ephraim and turned them back to the Lord, the God of
their ancestors.
—2 Chronicles 19:4

Asa worked hard to restore Israel to faith. He cleaned
the land of idols, rebuilt the kingdom infrastructure
and restored the worship of God. In his commitment
to eradicate false religion, he determined to kill
anyone who turned away from worshipping God.

He made a compelling argument for church at-
tendance, to be sure!

Interestingly, years later when one of God's
prophets called him out for sin in his own life, he did

not repent. Instead Asa turned with the same ferocity against God's messengers; it did not end well for him.

Jehoshaphat, on the other hand, determined to woo his people back to God when they drifted away. He established judges to disciple and instruct the people in God's law and consistently demonstrated humility.

If I'm perfectly honest, I have to confess my own heart's inclination toward the Asa school of revival. When I grow impatient with someone or some group of people, I have to remind myself how much God loves them. Grace, not the guillotine, is God's weapon of choice with wayward disciples. It is generally the case that encouragement, not a judgmental attitude, moves people forward in their faith.

What prompts us to incline toward Asa rather than Jehoshaphat in our ministry role? I have a suspicion. A few years ago, frustrated with my critical spirit, I sought help. A spiritual mentor helped me recognize that fear was the source of my sin. The remedy for fear and its consequences was simple: love. "Perfect love casts out fear" (1 John 4:18 ESV).

This insight has helped me pause whenever a critical spirit begins to well up in me. I ask myself what I am afraid of. Armed with the resultant insight, I can move past my fear and deal with the person or situation with God's grace and love instead of my own anxiety.

Choosing to love those who opposed me or whom I *perceived* to somehow threaten me went a long way toward displacing my Asa mindset with an attitude more like Jehoshaphat's.

What role do power and intimidation play in the way you lead? After answering this yourself, ask someone you know will speak honestly with you to answer this question from their perspective.

Water or Gasoline?

A gentle answer turns away wrath,
but a harsh word stirs up anger.
—Proverbs 15:1

Years ago I was on the staff of a church that was breaking apart. Summary dismissals, power plays, and emerging factions threatened to destroy the church community. It fell to me to preach the Sunday when the key decisions were announced and we fully expected an explosive response.

I explained to the congregation that each of them had two buckets in hand: one full of water, one full of gasoline. Fires were going to break out in the aftermath of the decision—rumors, character assassinations, calls to fight—and each of us would have to decide whether to put out those fires with water or feed them with gasoline. It wasn't going to be a one-time decision, I explained; we would be making this choice several times each day.

By God's grace the church body overwhelmingly responded with water. Almost all those who chose to remain—as well as the majority of those who felt compelled to leave—opted to act with grace toward one another. It was not a painless season by any means, but I think our testimony in the community remained intact.

As American Christians we find ourselves in a similar position today.

In the present political environment, it somehow satisfies our flesh to excoriate the politicians we do not support—and all those who are in their camp. Too many of us embrace scorn and mockery, and our words pump additional toxins into the poisonous atmosphere.

Scripture invites us to consider another possibility: grace. We listen for words we can cheer, we celebrate expressions of collaboration and common effort. When conversations turn personal and mean-spirited, we walk away or humbly encourage people to criticize ideas without personalizing the disagreement.

Depending on the situation, it may even be appropriate to offer alternative ways of looking at the person in question.

No, I'm not naive, and no, I don't believe we should ignore evil speech, evil laws, or whatever. But I don't think fanning the flames of uncivil discourse will achieve the righteousness of God. It is incumbent upon Christians to offer another way forward as a country, a way that "speaks truth in love" and models respect and love for those with whom we disagree.

The future does *not* belong to me; it belongs to my children and grandchildren. My responsibility is to show them how to live proactively and biblically in a world that sometimes disappoints and occasionally turns toxic. I want to show them how to pour water on fire rather than gasoline—and, when fire wins a round, how to rebuild out of the ashes in a spirit of grace.

Do my words kill, or do they bring life and reflect Jesus to my listeners?

God's Four-Letter Words: Obey

Jesus Christ our Lord, through whom we have received
grace and apostleship to bring about the obedience of
faith for the sake of his name among all the nations.
—Romans 1:4b–5 (ESV)

Does God cuss? No, but some of God's values can
sound like "four-letter words" to us, can't they?

For example, the word *obey* has fallen on hard
times. Our popular culture arches its back at any
suggestion that we have a responsibility to obey
(submit, follow) or line up with the will of another.
To post-modern ears *obey* is a four-letter word: ob-
scene and offensive. Yet in Romans 1, Paul says his
ministry—and hence ours as well—has the goal of
obedience at its core.

Once verse 5, previously overlooked, had my attention, I noticed *obey* and *obedience* popping up con-
tinuously in Romans—about twelve times. Several
of those occur in chapter 6, culminating in verse 17:
"But thanks be to God, that you who were once slaves
of sin have become obedient from the heart to the

standard of teaching to which you were committed" (ESV).

I love the phrase "obedient from the heart." It captures why Paul can link grace and obedience in describing his apostleship. We tend to think of grace and obedience as concepts that inhabit separate universes, but not Paul. Why is that?

The one who understands grace and what Jesus has purchased for us by his blood does not consider obedience an obligation or a duty. When we grasp the profound cost of the gift of salvation, obedience—or alignment with God's will—is a love-response, a high privilege.

This explains why Paul talks about his apostleship in terms of obedience, not just intellectual assent. Those who hear and believe obey as well.

And do so gladly.

Do I seek to understand the will of God in order to obey it? Does my obedience to Jesus reflect fear of being caught or punished, or deep gratitude for all he has done?

God's Four-Letter Words: Hope

Brothers and sisters, we do not want you to be
uninformed about those who sleep in death, so that
you do not grieve like the rest of mankind, who have no
hope.
—1 Thessalonians 4:13

For the grace of God has appeared that offers salvation
to all people. It teaches us to say "No" to ungodliness
and worldly passions, and to live self-controlled, upright
and godly lives in this present age, while we wait for the
blessed hope—
the appearing of the glory of our great God
and Savior, Jesus Christ,
—Titus 2:11–13

No, God does not cuss, but God frequently resorts to
a number of four-letter words that can make a grown
man cover his hears. We have already considered *obey*;
now we consider *hope*.

Hope does not have a sterling reputation at the
moment. For many today it smacks of wishing as opposed to doing, or perhaps promises without content.
In the church hope is often connected with faith in a
way that is unhelpful to both. What do I mean?

Just as faith is often cast as believing the unbelievable or believing without any rational basis, many perceive hope as dreaming for something better against all reason. Yet in Scripture faith and hope are *not* terms rooted in baseless or mindless belief against all reason; rather, they stand on the complete trustworthiness of God's historical relationship with us.

Consider how Paul defines the basis of our hope. Paul appeals to the concrete historical reality of the resurrection. Because Jesus died and rose again, we can believe he will do the same with us (1 Thessalonians 4:14). In Thessalonians 4:15 Paul stands on "the Lord's word." What "word" might that be? I think it is probably John 14:1-3, among other passages.

Notice that Paul does not tie hope to a particular circumstance or turn of events in our personal lives. Instead, Paul looks to Christ's return and the unveiling of the "the glory of our great God and Savior, Jesus Christ" (Titus 2:13) as the focus of our hope. If I could, I would insert the "Hallelujah Chorus" here!

Think about it. Paul is writing to a young church, a suffering church, and he does not tell them their hope is in the alleviation of their suffering—though that may happen. It is in the ultimate capstone of history, the return of our Savior, Redeemer, and Friend!

So hope may be a four-letter word for our friends and neighbors who do not know Jesus yet, but for us it is the wellspring of our confidence. It is the source of our strength in the midst of persecution, rejection, or suffering. Our joy flows from our hope in the promise given to us by the Resurrected One who promises to return for the Father's glory—and for us.

Do I live a life that reflects belief in Jesus' resurrection and confidence in Jesus' return?

God's Four-Letter-Words: Pray

Pray continually.
—1 Thessalonians 5:17

This is one of those verses kids love to memorize because it's so short. Yet for those of us who want to grow in our faith and practice, these are menacing words. We wonder who can keep them.

Maybe what we are asking is, Who can pray every waking hour and still get anything done? The question has two answers, and both deserve our attention.

First, we have to understand what the words in the verse mean. They do *not* mean ceaseless prayer. What they *do* mean is that prayer should be a constant practice in our daily lives.

Second, the very question—Who can pray and still get anything done?—presupposes that prayer is wasted time that produces nothing. In other words, it assumes every hour spent praying is one less hour dedicated to producing results. In contrast, I would propose it facilitates *all* ministry.

So Paul exhorts this young church to make prayer a priority, an ongoing part of church life.

True confession: It pains me to write the above words, because I periodically allow myself to become as busy as anyone, leaving prayer as a fitful and haphazard exercise. The cumulative effect of my prayerlessness always leaves me feeling drained.

By the time I turn away from my self-inspired planning and busywork, I feel completely out of my league ministry-wise. Why wouldn't I? After all, when ministry relies on *my* great ideas instead of God's leading and power, I have nothing to give and no hope of fruit.

Once I come to my senses, I find time to be with God and to listen. God is gracious, and once I begin "wasting time with God" again, I find real solutions to the struggles I face. Also, my prayer time revives me and refreshes my soul.

So why do we so easily drift away and fall back into old habits? I don't know; perhaps entropy? Arrogance? Procrastination? Lack of discipline? Whatever the answer, the fact is that the sooner we return to the practice of prayer, the sooner we enjoy fellowship with God and meaningful ministry with people.

Is prayer foundational in my daily life or an afterthought? What can I accomplish more effectively without God's guidance than with it?

God's Four-Letter-Words: Give

> Each one must give as he has decided in his heart,
> not reluctantly or under compulsion, for God loves a
> cheerful giver.
> —2 Corinthians 9:7 (ESV)

> Remember the words of the Lord Jesus, how he himself
> said, "It is more blessed to give
> than to receive."
> —Acts 20:35b (ESV)

> Truly, I tell you, this poor widow has put in more than
> all of them.
> —Luke 21:3 (ESV)

If ever a word from God offended human ears, *give* is that word. Gathering, keeping, guarding—we do these well. Giving from our storehouses? Giving *everything*? Not so much.

We have plenty of folk wisdom to justify us: "a penny saved is a penny earned," "save up for a rainy day," and "God helps those who help themselves."

John Wesley, the brilliant eighteenth- century evangelist, had another perspective: "Earn as much as you can, save as much as you can, give away as much as you can." Wesley understood the issue—we are stewards of God's resources, not the owners.

And those resources include much more than just money: time, presence, listening ears, compassion, respect, spiritual gifts. What the poor widow mostly gave at the temple was *devotion*, not money. She gave God *all* her devotion.

But stating that we are merely stewards may communicate something negative about giving. God does not intend our giving to cause us grief. Giving is a joy and a blessing. Giving is an expression of gratitude, not a burdensome duty.

After his encounter with Jesus and the gospel, Zacchaeus's first act is a lavish outpouring of his wealth (Luke 19), targeting the poor and those he had despoiled through corruption. I think God intended for us to live like Zacchaeus: joyfully generous, inspired by confidence in God and the pleasure of blessing others.

When giving includes sacrifice, am I quick to make excuses? Do I resent the object of my giving or even resent God? Do I see giving as a burden or a privilege?

God's Four-Letter Words: Love

You have heard that it was said, "Love your neighbor
and hate your enemy." But I tell you, love your enemies
and pray for those who persecute you, that you may be
children of your Father in heaven. He causes his sun
to rise on the evil and the good, and sends rain on the
righteous and the unrighteous. If you love those who
love you, what reward will you get? Are not even the tax
collectors doing that?
—Matthew 5:43–46

But God demonstrates his own love for us in this:
While we were still sinners, Christ died for us.
—Romans 5:8

You may be thinking *love* is the least offensive of
God's four-letter words. How could love offend
anyone? I suspect it offends us more than any of the
other words.

For one thing, it undergirds the reason we practice the other four-letter words—*obey, pray, hope,* and
give. They are all love responses. Also, God's love calls
us far beyond the realm of simply being nice to nice
people. Jesus suggests such expressions of feeling are
merely normal human transactions. God's definition

of love is much tougher than mutual back pats among buddies.

Who hates you (and whom do you hate)? Who causes you frustration? Who has hurt you? God calls us to love them. You see what I mean.

Now God does not mean we should return to the evildoer and remain their victim—that is insanity or masochism, not love. God *does* want us to see them as human, to seek the image of God in them (Matthew 25:40), and to engage that image within healthy boundaries.

God invites us to love divinely, to say no to politician bashing, hating, racism, sexism, arrogance, blanket condemnation of the other—whoever the "other" may be.

I knew a missionary who lived in a rural village with no water. Women in the village had to hike down to a ravine each day to fill jugs with water. It was an onerous task no one looked forward to. A neighbor woman hated my friend and treated my friend's children cruelly. My friend cried out to God in despair, and God told her to hike to the river and bring the woman a jug of water. She did.

My friend knocked at the woman's door, and when the woman appeared, her face full of hate, my friend gave her the jug. "This is for you," she said. The woman began weeping. This act of sacrificial love broke through the hatred. Soon after this the woman became a follower of Jesus.

No, it doesn't always work that way. But that doesn't matter.

Who has loved me when I did not deserve it? Am I with-holding love from anyone because they are different?

Pruning

I am the true vine, and my Father is the gardener. He
cuts off every branch in me that bears no fruit, while
every branch that does bear fruit he prunes so that it
will be even more fruitful.

—John 15:1–2

We made the three-hour trip from Guatemala City
to Chiquimula countless times over the course of our
fourteen years there. One small stretch of highway
I enjoyed ran past the town of Usutlán. Huge trees
reached over the road at that point and created a
shady canopy and brief respite from the tropical sun.
It was a quiet strip of road—no people, no activity,
just trees and shade.

After about eight years of road trips, a small kiosk appeared on the side of the road with a one-word
sign: GRAPES. I paid it no mind. Guatemalans *love*
grapes, but back then all the grapes consumed there
were imported; I figured this was just an enterprising
local trying to make a buck.

A couple of years went by; suddenly the trees of Usutlán provided shade for dozens of vendors selling grapes by the side of the road!

One day I decided to investigate, so I stopped at the original kiosk. The young lady who sold me my grapes explained what had happened. "My dad wanted to try growing grapes. He managed to get a small crop—but just enough to sell here by the road. It occurred to him that the Israelis are great farmers, so he asked their embassy for help. The agriculturalist who came showed my dad how to prune the vines. That year the harvest was six times larger! We planted more vines and continued improving our pruning methods, and now the harvests are huge. All these vendors sell what my father grows."

I suspect we all know several people whom God is pruning at present. It hurts. I think our friends would even say it feels like God is taking from them, stripping them. Yet the Vinedresser would explain it another way: "I am removing everything that is not really you and leaving you more you than before. Now you will have no sucker branches, no diseased twigs, no leaf rust. Instead I will have a cleaner, stronger branch able to bear much fruit."

When it's my turn for pruning, do I dodge the pruning shears or abide and trust God to do his work in me?

Sojourners

For the assembly, there shall be one statute for you
and for the stranger who sojourns with you, a statute
forever throughout your generations. You and the
sojourner shall be alike before the LORD.
—Numbers 15:15 (ESV)

He executes justice for the fatherless and the widow,
and loves the sojourner, giving him food and clothing.
Love the sojourner, therefore, for you were sojourners
in the land of Egypt.
—Deuteronomy 10:18–19 (ESV)

I cannot solve the immigration debate in a few
paragraphs or with a couple of Bible verses. However,
the texts above should encourage us to pray, listen,
and engage each other on this subject with more
humility than hubris.

Numbers 15 mentions sojourners multiple
times. The gist of God's exhortation? Treat them like
you treat yourselves. What a concept. It reminds me
of what Another said: "Do unto others as you would
have others do unto you" (Luke 6:31 MEV).

God tells us in Deuteronomy 10 to *love* the sojourner. No, I do not think this means we cannot or should not have borders or laws or values we hold, but it *does* mean we should begin our conversations on the subject with love—costly, self-sacrificing love. What does that look like?

Self-sacrificing love means approaching sojourners with grace and dignity. It means we remember in the course of debate that we are talking about human beings made in the image of God. Whatever framework of laws and guidelines we promote, we can agree that enforcement should reflect our best selves.

It also means we remember that those who disagree with us in this debate are *also* made in the image of God—therefore deserving of grace and respect. Reducing our opponents to "racists" or "bleeding hearts" so we can dismiss them out of hand without a hearing is sin. The biblical reminder that we should be "quick to hear, slow to speak, slow to anger" (James 1:19 ESV) applies well here.

The present debate in our country about immigration is not just about finding a solution; it is about the *way* we find a solution. Followers of Jesus should set the example.

Am I a voice for grace and humility and wisdom from above (James 3:17)? What can I do to bring a reconciling witness and meaningful solution to the public debate?

God's Anointed (Part 1)

Is anyone among you sick? Let him call for the elders of
the church, and let them pray over him, anointing him
with oil in the name of the Lord.
—James 5:14 (ESV)

As a pastor, as an elder, as a church leader, you have
probably been asked on more than one occasion to
pray for the sick. Perhaps you have asked yourself,
"What about the oil?"

Typically we hear one of three responses: (1) well,
that was a ritual for James's time and culture, so we
don't need to do that today; (2) the first century folk
viewed oil as a healing ointment, but today we take
our meds and pray; or (3) well, we don't really know
why God wants us to do it, but it is a biblical instruction, so we do it.

The passages above tell us another reason. In
Scripture, the anointing of oil is always an expression
of consecration, that is, *divine ownership*. In other
words, when we choose to anoint the sick before we
pray, we physically identify them as part of the "set
apart" community—those who belong to Jesus. We

anoint with oil to declare someone part of the royal priesthood (1 Peter 2:9), and with that we also emphasize the spiritual authority of our prayer.

The anointing is a witness to all powers and a reminder to the sick one and to ourselves: "This one is God's." I think that was what James was explaining to his early church readers—and to us. It's not so much the use of oil as the reminder of the *belonging* that matters.

There appears to be a further component to this ministry of praying for the sick. Notice the instruction calls for "the elders" to pray for the sick one. Certainly "the prayer of a righteous person has great power," according to James 5:16 (ESV), so why does James use the plural *elders*?

Could it be that the presence of a group of elders offers a picture of our belonging? In other words, do the elders provide a reminder to the sick brother or sister that they are part of a community that loves them and is upholding them? Our presence says to the one to whom we minister, "God has you, and so do we all; we are with you in this, and you are not alone."

To the one who is discouraged by their illness, the circle of elders becomes a concrete image of *all* God's people who care. This is an important reminder to those who feel alone in their sickness.

How does it impact my intercession to know the one for whom I pray belongs to God?

God's Anointed (Part 2)

Anoint the tabernacle and all that is in it ... so that it
may become holy.
—Exodus 40:9 (ESV)

There were twelve stones [on the breastplate] with their
names according to the names of the sons of Israel.
They were like signets, each engraved with its name, for
the twelve tribes.
—Exodus 39:14 (ESV)

They made the plate of the holy crown of pure gold,
and wrote on it an inscription, ... "Holy to the LORD."
And they tied to it a cord of blue to fasten it on the
turban.
—Exodus 39:30–31a (ESV)

In the previous reflection, we looked at the use of oil
for anointing those for whom we pray. I proposed the
anointing with oil served to remind both prayer and
prayed-for that the sick brother or sister belongs to
God.

There is more to the subject of anointing, however—much more. In Exodus 40:9, the Israelites
used anointing oil to consecrate (or "make holy") the

tabernacle, the tabernacle furniture, and the priests. The anointing oil identified each as exclusively God's and, therefore, set apart for God's purposes.

The high priest even wore a gold plate that declared him to be "holy to [set apart for] the Lord" (Exodus 39:30). In his role as the one Israelite set apart for God in order to mediate the work of redemption, only the high priest could enter the holy of holies, where the ark of the covenant rested.

All of the temple worship was symbolic—the holy of holies represented the very throne room of God, and when the high priest entered in, he symbolically brought Israel with him via the breastplate described in Exodus 39:14.

Now, however, the Holy Spirit abides in us—*we* are the tabernacle of God, God's holy place. As noted in the last reflection, Peter even describes us as "a royal priesthood, a holy nation, a people for his own possession." And to what end has God done all this? "That you may proclaim the excellencies of him who called you out of darkness into his glorious light" (1 Peter 2:9 ESV).

This description of how God sees us should give us pause. Often we reduce holiness to a set of behaviors by which we can measure how "holy" we are. However, holiness is not merely a list of dos and don'ts; it is a question of *identity*: Whose am I, and what is my purpose? We do not make ourselves holy;

rather, the fact that God has anointed us—filled us—
with his Holy Spirit makes us God's holy ones. Now,
in the Spirit's power, we can fulfill our purpose and
proclaim the excellencies of God to the world.

Have I acknowledged God's ownership of my entire life?
What part of my life have I tried to deny to God? What
in the world for?

God's Anointed (Part 3): Alive in Christ

Now there are varieties of gifts, but the same Spirit; and
there are varieties of service, but the same Lord. . . . For
just as the body is one and has many members, and all
the members of the body, though many, are one body, so
it is with Christ.

—1 Corinthians 12:4–5, 12 (ESV)

Some years ago one of my daughters taught me an important lesson from her high school freshman biology class—namely, all living things share six characteristics. Specifically, all living things:

1. Are organized (from cells on up there is structure)

2. Interact with their environment (they can't live isolated from their surroundings)

3. Reproduce (if not, they die out)

4. Adapt to their environment (or, again, they die out)

5. Metabolize (eat)

6. Possess stable internal conditions (which makes for a stable existence)

As individual followers of Jesus and as local bodies of believers, I think these six characteristics are also evident in us when we are healthy. Replace the phrase "all living things" with "all healthy Christians" or "all healthy churches," and you will see what I mean. These characteristics are the outworking of being an anointed and holy people.

The first four characteristics are self-evident in their application to us, but what about numbers five and six? "Eating" corresponds to a steady diet of prayer and reading God's Word. We will not flourish on a skimpy diet of Sunday worship and occasionally listening to Christian radio. We need to hunger and thirst for *God* and daily satisfy those longings (Matthew 5:6).

Internal stability is the outcome of living a life filled with the Holy Spirit and abiding in Jesus. *Stable* does not mean "unchanging." If we are alive in Christ, we will grow, we will develop, we will change. However, within the constant change provoked by our growth there is an internal centeredness that keeps our eyes focused on Jesus (Romans 12:1–2).

The previous two reflections focused on anointing and holiness. Well, the way it works itself out in the life of a believer is by making us fully alive—as per the six characteristics listed above. This is true for both individuals and church bodies.

When people watch me, do they see a spiritual zombie—or a bold and joyful follower of Jesus?

Weird for God

Now John was clad in camel's hair and wore a leather
belt around his waist and ate locusts and wild honey.
And he preached.
—Mark 1:6–7a (ESV)

Bible dialogues with non-Christians, or what some would call investigative Bible studies, are a regular part of my week. We use the first four chapters of Mark for that purpose. John the Baptist never fails to capture the attention of seekers.

Even in our increasingly post-Christian context, it seems most people have heard his name. However, when they encounter him in Scripture and learn about his lifestyle, they inevitably ask, "Why was he so weird?"

John does make the story of Jesus awkward in the telling. Yet Jesus loved him and declared, "Among those born of women there has arisen no one greater than John the Baptist" (Matthew 11:11 ESV). Jesus was not at all embarrassed by John.

Why not? Because John was sold out for the good news; he had bet the house on Jesus. He boldly embraced the mission God had given him to call all Israel to repentance in order to prepare the way for Jesus.

The French writer Gustave Flaubert captures the impact of John perfectly in his short story "Herodias" in the book *Three Tales*. For the protagonist, who had violated Jewish law to marry her husband's brother, King Herod Antipas, John

> was a thorn in her side. The speeches he had addressed to great crowds had spread far and wide, and were still circulating; she heard them repeated everywhere, and they filled the air. Faced with legions of troops, she would have been brave enough, but this intangible force was deadlier than the sword, and utterly perplexing.

John willingly preached even against the sin of ruling authorities, knowing the risks. Not in order to mock them. Not to magnify himself. But rather to call them to repent of their sin and draw near to God through the coming Messiah.

Weird indeed.

Frankly, if we consider pivotal eras in church history, we often find a weird character leading the charge. Someone who cares not for comfort or power or approval. Someone willing to lay aside *every* encumbrance in order to turn the heart of a people or a nation or an age.

Paul was weird. St. Patrick was weird. George Fox (my hero) was *really* weird. Martin Luther, John Wesley, Mary Slessor, Hudson Taylor, Amy Carmichael—all were found weird by the world's standards. Weird for God.

Could it be the only people God can use to attempt great things for the kingdom are the ones who give no thought to themselves?

When the world looks at me, do they see someone who is distressingly normal or someone who is "weird for God"?

First Things First

And when they had prayed, the place in which they
were gathered together was shaken, and they were all
filled with the Holy Spirit and continued to speak the
word of God with boldness.
—Acts 4:31 (ESV)

I hear Acts 4:32–35 quoted wistfully by Christians
who would *love* to see this spirit in our churches.
One cannot help but admire the generosity and self-
sacrifice of the Jerusalem Christians, as well as their
boldness and unity—what is not to admire? We ask
ourselves what keeps us from living equally passionate
lives. I think Luke offers us a clue.

"And when they had prayed. . . ." The Jerusalem
church was a praying church; it was a church birthed
out of a prayer meeting. Their ministry plan seems to
have been, "pray, be present in the city, and watch for
divine openings." Later on organization and structure
would evolve, but the movement itself was birthed
out of prayer.

Programs and planning are not intrinsically bad.
However, we cannot program generosity, sacrifice, or

bold witness. We cannot merely plan our way into revival. But we can pray our way into changed hearts—and prepared hearts—so that we can respond when the Spirit moves next. When the Spirit moves, then the planning and programming will have a purpose and a context.

Do you want to see new life in your church? Pray. Do you want to see your church making an impact in your community? Pray for God to create openings and then step into them as God reveals opportunities. Do you want to see people in your congregation taking initiative with unreached subcultures around you? Pray—and when God raises up volunteer ministers, be sure to affirm them, commission them, and celebrate their victories (not neglecting to encourage them in their defeats).

Prayer does not replace planning, organization, processes, or budgets; it precedes them. Do you want a church like the one in Jerusalem? First things first.

How convinced am I that prayer is the lifeblood of meaningful, lasting ministry? What one step could I take to further the role of prayer in my life and ministry?

Manipulation

> The man of God said, "I cannot turn back and go with
> you, nor can I eat bread or drink water with you in
> this place. I have been told by the word of the LORD:
> 'You must not eat bread or drink water there or return
> by the way you came.'" The old prophet answered, "I
> too am a prophet, as you are. And an angel said to me
> by the word of the LORD: 'Bring him back with you to
> your house so that he may eat bread and drink water.'"
> (But he was lying to him.)
> —1 Kings 13:16–18

I confess that this passage is one of those that has troubled me every year I come across it in my Bible reading. There is much that is confusing—and disturbing—in this text. Why, I wonder, did God ensure this story survived?

We do not know the names of the principal parties. We do not know why this self-centered prophet remained in Israel after Jeroboam instituted idolatry as the national religion and the vast majority of priests and Levites left Israel for Judah (2 Chronicles 11:13). The text does not tell us why this otherwise fearless and obedient "man of God" ignored his instructions and returned home with the old prophet. And we do not know why the old prophet lied. Or do we?

I think I finally understand a portion of what God wants to teach us in this passage. Actually, I think this passage has a *number* of lessons for the reader. I will stick with one: the high cost of manipulative leadership.

God gave the man of God clear instructions: Go. Prophecy against Jeroboam's altar and religion. Come right back. Do not eat or drink in the land nor go back the way you came.

He went. He prophesied. He refused the king's invitation to dine with him because of his instructions. He started home a different way.

But the old prophet wanted an audience with the man of God. Perhaps he longed for fellowship. Perhaps he longed for the legitimacy and influence that would come with hosting the man of God in his home. Whatever the reason, the prophet invited the man of God home, and the latter resisted because of his divine instructions.

The old man would not accept defeat; he appealed to his role as a prophet for legitimacy and then lied to the man of God, telling him, "an angel spoke to me by the word of the Lord, saying, 'Bring him back with you.'" The man of God followed the old prophet home and paid for the decision with his life.

Manipulation based on position—the abuse of influence. It is unbecoming of political leaders, but it is absolutely destructive when practiced by those who present themselves as servants of God. The older man manipulated in order to get what he wanted; he got it, and the young man (I don't know why, but I think of him as a younger man) suffered the consequences. The manipulator lured the victim into direct disobedience.

Perhaps the apostle Paul had this passage in mind when he warned the Galatian Christians against the temptation to return to the law for their salvation. Religious leaders had come to the church and were confusing the body with false teaching. These manipulators misused the Torah for their purposes similarly to how the old prophet claimed to have received a word from an angel. Paul warned the Galatians, "But even if we *or an angel from heaven* should preach a gospel other than the one we preached to you, let them be under God's curse" (Galatians 1:8, emphasis mine).

The lesson for us? When a leader or voice of influence seeks to manipulate us into beliefs or practices out of alignment with Scripture, we should keep walking—no matter what they claim to have heard from God. And woe to those leaders who destroy others through manipulation for their own purposes.

In my role as a leader, how intentional am I about pursuing the best interests of those whom I lead? What checks do I have in my life to guard me against manipulating others?

Praying Alone

When morning came, all the chief priests and the elders
of the people took counsel against Jesus to put him to
death.
—Matthew 27:1 (ESV)

Over coffee this week, a friend and I began a conversation about prayer and the value of drawing away to be alone with God. As a prayer exercise it has much to recommend it. And yet . . .

Why the pause? We began to recall the times Jesus went away to pray, and his experience did not always end, well, pleasantly.

Look at the book of Matthew, for example. In Matthew 4 Jesus goes into the wilderness to fast and pray, and Satan shows up. Time alone with the Father in this case triggers a contest with the evil one.

In chapter 14 Jesus goes away to pray after feeding the five thousand. We do not know what occurred on the mountaintop with the Father, but down on the lake, a storm erupted and terrified the disciples. On the positive side, Jesus had an opportunity to demonstrate his authority—perhaps fortified by time alone with the Father.

In Matthew 17 Jesus goes away but takes Peter, James, and John. Moses and Elijah join them, Jesus is transformed, and the disciples are dumbfounded. The experience is so glorious, Peter suggests they camp out there. Instead, Jesus returns them to a spiritual confrontation down on the plain.

In Matthew 26:36–47, Jesus takes the three with him and goes away to pray. The disciples fall asleep while Jesus pleads for relief. It appears no one shows up—except the temple guards and Judas. The Father remains silent.

Finally, there is the most sobering account of all. Beginning in Matthew 26:57, the guards march Jesus to the home of Caiaphas, where Peter denies him and his accusers buffet him. It is late, and Jesus' captors eventually lower him into the pitch-black cell beneath the high priest's home where he passes the rest of the night.

A few hours earlier, Jesus had washed the feet of the disciples and broke bread with them. Now, abandoned, beaten, judged, and consigned to a dark, muddy pit in complete darkness, he waits in solitude.

Jesus knew what would follow in the morning. What might he have prayed at that moment? Scripture does not tell us, but I suspect that in those hours Jesus fought his fiercest battles with Satan—and won.

What can we learn from these passages? (1) Going off alone to pray can be incredibly rich and satisfying; (2) it can be a place of spiritual war; (3) it is often a place of renewal and refreshment; and (4) it can be a place of great labor and sorrow. As children of the resurrection, we know one more truth: we are *never* alone. Listen: "In the same way, the Spirit helps us in our weakness. We do not know what we ought to pray for, but the Spirit himself intercedes for us through wordless groans" (Romans 8:26).

How meaningful a role does praying alone play in my own spiritual practices? Am I prepared to face any challenges that follow these seasons of prayer?

No Lack

The LORD is my shepherd; I shall not want.
—Psalm 23:1 (KJV)

Jehová es mi pastor; nada me faltará.
—Salmo 23:1 (RVR 1960)

As a spiritual exercise I once committed to read Psalm 23 daily and then to bring it to my mind for reflection throughout the day.

Since I had memorized this psalm years ago in Spanish as well as English, I thought I would use this opportunity to refresh my memory. Every morning, after reading the psalm, I recited it in both English and Spanish. Around day three a slight difference in emphasis in verse 1 caught my attention.

While both versions say the same thing, the phrasing in Spanish has an extra "kick" to it that I love. Instead of "I shall not want [lack]," the Spanish version phrases it, "*nothing* will I lack". In Spanish, word order is everything. Putting *nothing* at the start of the sentence adds an intentional emphatic boost to the meaning.

This phrase became my focus all week long in every situation and circumstance I encountered, whether my own or someone else's. Think about it: if I lack *nothing*, then I have whatever I need in every circumstance I face. God is enough when no one else is.

Whatever I am facing in my calling—and whatever you are facing in yours—God is enough. We have everything we need to negotiate the challenges, shortfalls, shortcomings, or disappointments of our ministry because "*nothing* will [we] lack."

During that week, when I had to review budgets—both personal and ministerial—and make adjustments for the year, this psalm reminded me that *nothing* would we lack. The Lord is our Shepherd—and has our back.

We also had to deal with some crushing news in the lives of some dear friends, disappointing behavior in one or two others, and potential threats of a spiritual or physical nature in the lives of others. While negotiating those circumstances, we were confronted repeatedly with our own insufficiency, but we were also reminded, "*Nothing* will [we] lack." In the midst of our own insufficiency, our Shepherd is fully sufficient!

"The Lord is my shepherd; *nothing* will I lack." When we keep this truth front and center in our minds, it makes all the difference in our journeys.

What circumstance am I in right now that confronts me with my inadequacy? Am I going it alone, or am I looking to God to provide what I need?

Against Rage

Jesus called them together and said, "You know that the
rulers of the Gentiles lord it over them, and their high
officials exercise authority over them. Not so with you.
Instead, whoever wants to become great among you
must be your servant."
—Matthew 20:25–26

We all recognize the new spirit afoot in our country.
The political left and right have made conflict and
fury an art form.

Reporting on someone taking offense at another has become a media staple, because outrage sells.
Sins of one's past (real or imagined) have become
career-enders. This spirit of the age makes reasoned
conversation about real ills almost impossible to
sustain. Instead of reason we appeal to rage. In the
present environment, convincing those with whom
we disagree is a waste of time; we must destroy them.

Faced with competing shrill voices on the airwaves, we are tempted to either dive into the brawl or
become more and more ambivalent about the "news."
For those of us with no interest in the ranting and

mockery, how can we stay engaged while responding proactively and gracefully?

We must first acknowledge the grim truth that periodically the nations rage and people cast off restraint—it is who we are. We will not fix the problem permanently, and we certainly will not improve the drama, if we play by the world's rules. So we must constantly remind ourselves that our battle is for hearts, not votes. How do we do that in the present environment?

The mission of the church has not changed in 2000 years: "Go and make disciples" (Matthew 28:19). Do not merely react to the world; go out and proactively proclaim *and live* the good news—not as political minions but as Spirit-compelled kingdom dwellers. Love one another, love the lost, love the political fringes, love the trampled. Capture hearts and minds with the life-changing, neighborhood-changing, society-changing message of Jesus.

What is Jesus' message for the church right now in this "age of rage"? The same as always: "I have not changed. My mission has not changed. Keep loving. Keep serving. Oh, and be of good cheer, for I have overcome the world."

Am I reacting to the world's raging or proactively reflecting Jesus in the midst of it?

A Shepherd Like That!

Your rod and your staff, they comfort me.
—Psalm 23:4b

During a season of meditation on Psalm 23, God gave me some fresh insights into the Shepherd who deepened my appreciation for Jesus.

The quote from Psalm 23:4 speaks to a shepherd's tools of the trade: a rod (think "club") and a staff. The former serves as a weapon to crumple predators or thieves with lamb chops on their minds. The latter aids the shepherd in bringing distracted sheep back into the flock.

Thus armed and equipped, the shepherd provides assurance and direction to the clawless, fangless, (might I add "dull-minded"?) sheep. While the shepherd remains, life continues undisturbed.

It struck me that *this* Shepherd described by David bears little resemblance to the Good Shepherd one sees in stained-glass church windows. The stained-glass Jesus usually stands alone, possibly with a staff in one hand. In the crook of the other arm, he carries a little lamb.

I do not intend to demean the picture I just described; I honestly like those windows and the message they communicate. All of us need the tender care of God at times, and the image of the lamb-carrying Christ reminds us that the arms of Jesus are always open. However, I think an armed-and-ready Jesus offers a more befitting picture that captures his central role in the life of God's children. Our—or at least *my*—main experience with Jesus seems to run more on the side of Defender and Shepherd. I generally find him either battling on my behalf or reeling me in.

In moments of spiritual battle, when we or the church are under attack, when God calls us to take strongholds—or cities—I think we find encouragement in knowing the rod-and-staff-carrying Shepherd goes before us. A Shepherd like that makes it possible for us to confidently declare, "Even though I walk through the valley of the shadow of death, I will fear no evil, for *you* are with me" (Psalm 23:4a ESV, emphasis mine).

Jesus with a club at the ready in one hand and a staff in the other may not be a common stained-glass theme, but he's a Shepherd I can follow!

How would it affect my willingness to take risks for God if I pictured Jesus as a Shepherd like that?

God's Garments

[God] put on righteousness as his breastplate,
and the helmet of salvation on his head;
he put on the garments of vengeance
and wrapped himself in zeal as in a cloak.
—Isaiah 59:17

Put on the full armor of God, so that you can take your
stand against the devil's schemes.
—Ephesians 6:11

Paul exhorted the Ephesians to "put on the full armor of God" in a clear reference to the Isaiah passage quoted above. The message Paul has for the church is clear: God's armor equips us for the life of faith.

In battle, armor fulfills two purposes, one defensive and one offensive These two purposes hold true for spiritual conflict as well. First, as a defensive measure, God's armor allows us to withstand the onslaught of Satan. However, God does not intend for us to merely absorb the enemy's blows; we also wear God's armor to go on the offensive and destroy the strongholds of the enemy (2 Corinthians 10:4).

Notice Paul did *not* ask the Ephesians to put on the "garments of God." The garments and the mantle of God are vengeance and fury—the working out of a holy God's wrath. In Isaiah 59 the prophet announces that God is done putting up with Israel's injustice, unrighteousness, spiritual blindness, iniquity, oppression, and disdain for the truth. Because no one could be found to turn the people away from their collective sin, God steps in and cleans up the mess (59:16). Dressed in vengeance and fury, God deals with the hard of heart in perfect holiness and righteousness— something we could never do. God's judgment sets up future restoration and reconciliation.

Paul does not invite the believers in Ephesus to put on God's garments, because wrath is reserved for God alone. Instead, Paul makes it clear in both Ephesians and 2 Corinthians that people are *not* the focus of our warfare. Powers, principalities, and the spiritual authorities of this present darkness are the appropriate targets of our ire. In the human realm, we hold fast to our ministry of reconciliation.

People—even those who attack or persecute us—are not the enemy. Let's not forget it.

What ongoing relationship causes me the most difficulty? Have I tried to approach it dressed in God's garments or God's armor?

Human Milkweed

Then Joseph said to his brothers . . . "I am your brother
Joseph, the one you sold into Egypt! And now, do not
be distressed and do not be angry with yourselves for
selling me here, because it was to save lives that God
sent me ahead of you."

—Genesis 45:4–5

[Frodo said,] "I do not feel any pity for Gollum. He
deserves death". [Gandalf replied,] "Deserves death!
I daresay he does. Many that live deserve death. And
some die that deserve life. Can you give that to them?
Then be not too eager to deal out death in the name of
justice."

—J.R.R. Tolkien, *The Two Towers*

Milkweed has always annoyed me. Do you know
which weed I am referring to—the one that appears
overnight and sends out long stems? If you do not
pull it out carefully, it breaks and covers your fingers
with milky, sticky liquid.

I am always on the hunt for these pests in the
garden. It gives me sinister satisfaction to identify

them and extract them like some kind of embedded floral terrorists.

Then recently I discovered they make a unique contribution to the ecology of our state: they provide the only feeding spot for monarch caterpillars. The monarch butterflies migrate from Mexico to California every year, and milkweed is crucial to the continuation of these gorgeous insects. Urbanization and, ahem, zealous gardeners, have drastically reduced their access to milkweed, and this has contributed to the decline of the monarch.

Armed with this information, Barb and I agreed to let the milkweed thrive, and lo and behold, monarchs have been showing up all over our garden. Ironic, isn't it? No annoying milkweed, no beautiful monarchs.

Some people in our lives offend us as deeply as milkweed in a garden; the boss who routinely criticizes us or perhaps a toxic neighbor or discouraging coworker. Some, like Joseph's brothers, may even try to destroy us. Life would be much easier without them. We may even begin thinking, like Frodo, that life would be better if they were dead.

Yet God often uses these people in our lives. Yes, even them—in my life and in yours. It may be in some very direct way: sharpening us, pushing us to greater dependency on God. Or it may be in an unanticipated fashion: redirecting our course or impeding us in some manner that God uses redemptively.

Weeds that bless. Difficult people God uses to shape or direct us. Who knew?

What circumstance or person in my life am I trying to escape? What is God doing in me through this challenge?

Coming and Going

Come to me, all you who are weary and burdened, and I
will give you rest.
—Matthew 11:28

Therefore go and make disciples of all nations,
baptizing them in the name of the Father and of the
Son and of the Holy Spirit.
—Matthew 28:19

An ongoing conversation among pastors and church
planters has to do with the question, How do we
reach people? The camps align behind two opposing
banners: attractional versus missional ministry.

Those in the former group emphasize inviting
people to visit on a Sunday or to come to a special
event. Church members are encouraged to invite unsaved friends, neighbors, or coworkers. The key word
is *come*—as in Matthew 11:28 or John 1:39.

Missional churches "hate to wait." These congre-
gations emphasize entering the world of the unsaved
and engaging them where they are. These believers

focus on the world go. These ministers rally around Matthew 28:19 and Acts 1:8.

Proponents of each view have spilt much ink over this debate. In a recent conversation with the mission pastor of a church in LA, I gleaned an insight on this subject. Jesus says both "come" and "go"! He did both. At times, Jesus invited people into his circle (the disciples, the rich young ruler), but at other times we find Jesus *going* to the lost, as when he went to Zacchaeus or the inhabitants of the Decapolis.

So perhaps we do not face an either-or proposition. Perhaps attractional and missional strategies provide examples of *corporate* and *personal* obedience to Jesus and his mission. In other words, "come" is the *corporate* commitment to reaching and discipling others—the emphasis of the gathered church. A church that plans invitations to the community *and* also has pathways to disciple those who do come is probably going to see much fruit.

Proponents of the missional viewpoint do not want to wait for people to show up. They want to *go* and find lost folk and make disciples. It's a *personal* commitment. Their attitude demonstrates our individual responsibility to engage lost people in our corner of the world. We share, we pray, we invite them into Bible dialogues—we bring Jesus into their world.

Both strategies seek to reach lost people; both groups want to obey Jesus. Jesus did both. So as the body of Christ, it makes sense to tell people to come, but as individuals we go into the space, the community, of those who are not ready to enter into ours.

Am I committed to both coming and going? How are they manifested in my life?

Unforgivable

And I will pour out on the house of David and
the inhabitants of Jerusalem a spirit of grace and
supplication. They will look on me, the one they have
pierced, and they will mourn for him.
—Zechariah 12:10a

Over the past few years, the press has discovered a
new growth industry: digging up misdeeds from one's
past and confronting the sinner with the evidence.
Musicians, producers, priests, politicians—even
prime ministers—have found themselves in the hot
seat. I caught part of a conversation on the radio in
which a reporter interviewed an author whose book
examines the impact of digital photographic records
on our public reputations.

The interviewer asked if past actions that occurred in a different age or perhaps in one's youth
should be held to the same standard as present-day
actions. "In other words . . ." here the journalist hesi-
tated. "Are some actions simply unforgivable?"

Using the Prime Minister of Canada as an example (an old photo of him dressed as Aladdin with

darkened skin recently surfaced), the author responded, "Some things can be chalked up to youthful stupidity, but what he did? Yes, it is unforgivable."

Unforgivable.

No restoration.

What struck me in the exchange was the cold hardness of this new breed of secular justice. It is justice unclouded by doubt, justice unmediated by grace.

In the book of Zechariah, God speaks of a new future for Israel. This blessed future will not be earned by Israel. In fact, God's grace will precede Israel's repentance and even make it possible. Zechariah tells his audience that they will turn their backs on the Messiah and crucify him. This same Israel that had previously rejected God will reject the Word made flesh at a future time.

Unforgivable? No. Indeed, Zechariah declares that God will not wait for Israel to come to her senses. Notice: "I will pour out . . . a spirit of grace and supplication . . . and they will mourn for him" (Zechariah 12:10). God always makes the first move toward us who have sinned.

The one Being who has the right to declare us unforgivable instead declares, "Forgiven!" The One who should turn his back instead tells us, "Here I am! I stand at the door and knock" (Revelation 3:20).

Is there anyone I have declared unforgivable? How should I pray for them—and for myself?

You've Changed!

So from now on we regard no one from a worldly point
of view. Though we once regarded Christ in this way,
we do so no longer. Therefore, if anyone is in Christ, the
new creation has come:
The old has gone, the new is here!
—2 Corinthians 5:16–17

How does it happen that one can read a passage over and over—even memorize it—and still miss the main point for decades? Suddenly, a light clicks on and we catch what we have missed in multiple readings. This has happened to me several times this year, and occurred again while reading 2 Corinthians 5.

Verse 17 is one of those core verses Christians memorize for assurance or to inspire new Christians to hold on in the face of self-doubt. I have memorized it (and the following verses) in English, Spanish, and Indonesian; preached it in churches; and reflected on it privately many times.

With all that, I never caught the connection with verse 16 until this week. My teaching on the passage was accurate as far as it went—God does make us new; God does give us the ministry of reconciliation—but my understanding was incomplete.

While verse 17 and the following verses do re-assure us of our position in Christ, it is verse 16 that frames the passage and its meaning. Notice: "So from now on we regard *no one* from a worldly point of view" (emphasis mine). Why? Because of this declaration in verse 15: "He died for all, that those who live should no longer live for themselves but for him." Therefore (from our new perspective), "if anyone is in Christ, he is a new creation."

Paul calls the Corinthian church—and *us*—to look at one another as the new creations that we have become. Paul wants us to think the best of one another, to want the best for each other, to hope the best for one another. Why? Because we've changed!

We are not just new creations in God's eyes; we should see each other this way as well!

What fellow Christian taxes my patience or provokes my anger? How might I change the dynamic by seeing them as a new creation and engaging them in light of that understanding?

Comfort and Control

As a dog returns to its vomit,
so fools repeat their folly.
—Proverbs 26:11

I have never heard a sermon preached on the above verse, but I have experienced its bitter truth in my own life occasionally.

Under the demands of the past few weeks, I found myself falling back into some behaviors I had not seen in myself in many years. Specifically, I refer to a style of communication that hurts or frustrates others who have to work with me.

I assumed I had triumphed over these character flaws years ago and did not have to worry about them anymore. Yet when stress mounted in my work, I promptly retrieved them from my "spiritual attic" and rolled them back out into polite society.

They worked as poorly this time as they had before. Rather than inspiring anyone to greater performance, they only added to the chaos until I repented, made things right with my victims, and reflected on what had happened. Later I had coffee with a friend who has spent years in recovery. My friend shared how addicts and the children of addicts use "comfort and control" to deal with stress and anxiety.

A light went on: comfort and control—that's me! Running roughshod over people to control outcomes.

He continued, "We think if we can just work hard enough to finish all our projects, then life will be perfect." How many times had I told myself that in the past weeks? Guess what? It never happens. Still, I work overtime, push others, and squeeze margins in the vain hope of "getting it all done."

Comfort and control.

So what happened to the "victory" I thought I had achieved over my character flaws? Well, it wasn't totally fake—margins and choosing where to invest my efforts had kept me relatively balanced. However, I took on too much, and instead of lowering my expectations, I increased them. This was my *modus operandi* in the bad old days, and it produced the same results.

"As a dog returns to his vomit. . . ."

The good news? When I repented I encountered grace. When I apologized I found forgiveness. When I embraced margins and limits, I encountered rest and renewal. And God dealt with the rest of my anxiety as well. Again.

Here is another verse I like better: "Therefore I tell you, do not worry about your life, what you will eat or drink; or about your body, what you will wear. Is not life more than food, and the body more than clothes?" (Matthew 6:25).

Where in my life have I abandoned trust in God for comfort and control?

Casting Mountains

> For truly I tell you, if you have faith the size of a
> mustard seed, you will tell this mountain, "Move from
> here to there," and it will move.
> —Matthew 17:20 (CSB)

> Probably no admonition of Jesus has been more
> difficult to follow than the command to "love your
> enemies."
> —Martin Luther King, *Strength to Love*

I have been dwelling on Matthew 17:20 all week. It began when I had one of those periodic encounters we all have with a difficult individual. As God would have it, as this person began making life difficult for me, Matthew 17 showed up in my daily reading.

I have always applied this mountain-moving passage to the world around me. That is, I picture myself praying and changing other situations or other people—funding comes through for a project, a person is healed, a government decision goes "our way." So my immediate response when I read this passage was to pray, "*Yes!* Lord, cast this person into the sea!"

(Figuratively, not literally.) The heavenly silence was deafening.

God turned it around on me. "What if," I found myself asking, "God wants to cast *me* into the ocean? What if the mountain God wants to move is *my* attitude, *my* actions?" Well, that was an uncomfortable conversation, as you can imagine. The point of it was, "Alan, don't worry about the other person; I want to change you. I want to cast your self-righteousness and presumption into the sea and replace them with a loving, forgiving heart."

Like Jonah, I had to ask to be thrown into the "sea of repentance"—along with my ego and personal agendas. This may surprise you, but God does not care about our personal agendas. The good news? God heard my prayer and extracted the contentiousness out of my heart, replacing it with love for my challenging friend and a commitment to exercise grace.

What "mountain" is there in your own life that needs to be prayed into the ocean?

It's All Good

Now I want you to know, brothers and sisters, that
what has happened to me has actually served to advance
the gospel. As a result, it has become clear throughout
the whole palace guard and to everyone else that I am in
chains for Christ.
—Philippians 1:12–13

One of my favorite A. W. Tozer quotes says, "When
the Bible tells us 'all things work together for good'
it means 999 out of a 1000 . . . plus one." Tozer was
right, of course. The church will not be stopped by
pandemics, wars, or social upheaval—and may even
take on new life in the midst of them.

Church historians tell us social dislocation of
some kind often precedes revival. Why might that
be? I think it takes major upheaval for us humans to
acknowledge that our ways are not working. Also,
in the midst of chaos we Christians seem to recen-
ter ourselves spiritually and recover our first love for
God—and a passion for serving and sharing Jesus
with others.

During the early months of the COVID-19 crisis, I heard many people talking about and struggling with the constraints of the "new normal." For the record, I was first among sinners. I was not accustomed to camping within the four walls of our house. However, the constraint *did* cause me to reflect on what life in prison—especially solitary confinement—might feel like and what a grievous punishment it is to have one's freedom taken away.

In a very small way, I experienced something of what Paul endured on a regular basis. Yet Paul, writing from a prison cell in Rome to the church in Philippi (where he also spent time in prison), rejoiced in his circumstances! Paul did not see himself as a prisoner; rather, he looked at everyone around him as a "captive audience," if you will.

The obligation to forego Sunday morning worship during the crisis gave birth to a burst of creativity among Christians. We explored new ideas on outreach, new opportunities for service, and new partnerships among churches and ministries. A fresh breeze stirred among us. In individual households I even saw families taking a greater responsibility for their spiritual formation (good news, indeed!).

Caesar put Paul in prison to constrain him; instead, the entire palace guard (and the rest of the palace community) heard the gospel. COVID-19 put all of us under house detention, and yet. . . .

In seasons of dislocation, do I retreat in fear, or do I look for opportunities that God has prepared for me and my household—for me and my church?

The Morning After

Then the two told what had happened on the way, and
how Jesus was recognized by them
when he broke the bread.
—Luke 24:35

I think for many of us the Easter account generally ends with the resurrection. Jesus reveals himself to the disciples, Satan is defeated—game over. If you think about it, the gospel silence after the resurrection is thunderous; aside from the first encounters with Jesus, we hear little of the post-resurrection events. What happened afterward? Well, we catch a glimpse in Luke 24:13–35.

Cleopas and the other disciple leave Jerusalem on Sunday morning and have a dramatic encounter with Jesus on the road to Emmaus. How dramatic? Jesus meets them along the way, converses with them, and ultimately reveals himself to them as he breaks bread for them. In response they bolt from the inn and race back to Jerusalem to tell the good news to the others. Just hours before, these same two disciples had dismissed the report of the women about Jesus' resurrection.

The morning after Easter marks the start of our part in God's story, God's mission. Easter—the resurrection—is not the end of the story; we should think of it as the starting pistol for *our* race, our mission as the church.

Like the women who went to the garden, like the disciples on the road to Emmaus, we now have good news to share:

> He himself bore our sins in his body on the tree, that we might die to sin and live to righteousness. By his wounds you have been healed.
>
> (1 Peter 2:24 ESV)

May our own hearts burn within us.

In this post-Easter world, with whom can I share good news today?

Prophets or Priests

> Eli's sons were scoundrels; they had no regard for the
> LORD.... for they were treating the LORD's offering
> with contempt.
> —1 Samuel 2:12, 17b

Eli was a priest, a descendent of Aaron the brother of Moses. His sons, by virtue of being part of the tribe of Levi, were priests as well. They were also scoundrels. They seduced (or raped—the text doesn't make it clear) women who served at the tabernacle (2:22); they took the part of the sacrifice that corresponded to God, because they preferred God's portion to their own (2:29); and they refused to boil the priestly portion as prescribed by the law, because they wanted their meat barbecued (2:15). As the Scripture quoted above puts it, they "treated the offering of the Lord with contempt."

This happens. We have a tendency to confuse position with anointing. Tribal affiliation did not make a priest; God's anointing did. Seminaries do not make ministers; God does. A title does not make one a priest or a pastor or an elder or a teacher; God's call does that. But Eli and his sons had forgotten that titles only have meaning if the power of God stands behind the title.

Eli thought he could make his sons priests, and, I suppose, in some fashion he succeeded. They had the robes, they had the title, and they knew the procedures. When people sacrificed at the tabernacle, Eli's sons showed up. But they were "worthless men" who had no clue who God was or what the sacrificial system represented. They were merely titleholders—priests practicing a trade for their own advantage.

Samuel did not start out as a priest, but he was consecrated to God from birth by his parents. God called Samuel while he was still a child and gave him a mission; Samuel obeyed. You see, although Samuel was indeed a Levite by birth (see 1 Chronicles 6:16ff), he did not become a priest until he first became a prophet. He became a prophet once he knew God.

Why does this matter? Although seminaries and roles have their place, we can easily become preoccupied with obtaining titles and diplomas. We assume that a diploma or a job title will confer upon us spiritual authority even though we have not had a transformative encounter with God. It does not work that way. Ministry that matters births out of knowing God, hearing God's call, and embracing God's invitation. The other stuff follows.

May we all become prophets who know God's voice, God's calling.

Have I heard God's call on my own life? Am I still listening?

Our Moment?

Then Peter stood up with the Eleven, raised his voice
and addressed the crowd.
—Acts 2:14a

When they had got me out, they beat me exceedingly,
threw me down, and turned me
over a hedge.
—George Fox, *The Journal of George Fox*

I was teaching a course on church history. As part of
the course homework, I asked the students to read
through the book of Acts three times, so I thought I
should read it as well. That exercise, together with our
study of the expansion of the church, prompted me to
write the following words in my journal:

Peter preached and thousands converted.
Peter and John preached and were sent to
jail. Stephen preached and was murdered.
Paul preached and was beaten, stoned, imprisoned, and mocked. Fox preached and
started a movement. Wesley preached and
changed a nation. I preach and people tell

me I'm nice. Maybe I'm not all that nice if my words lack provocation and conviction?

What is the use of being "nice" when people are lost and looking for answers, if I ignore them? We presently find ourselves in a situation not of our own making. We stand in it as servants of God Almighty, as sons and daughters of the Father—as actors, not as victims.

The Chinese word for *crisis* is composed of two other words: *danger* and *opportunity*. In one sense, it does not matter how we arrived here; what matters more is our response to the situation in which we find ourselves.

When we launched North County Project to evangelize cities in North Orange County, we determined that one of our core values was "boldness inspired by gratitude." Peter, John, Stephen, Martin Luther, George Fox, John Wesley, William Carey, Gladys Aylward, Elizabeth Elliot—all embraced the danger of their calling. They chose to seize their ministry opportunities with all the risks, inspired by their gratitude for what God had done in their lives. I want to stand with them in my ministry.

Father, how do you want to use me today for your glory and the healing of fearful, wounded souls?

Open Doors

A great door for effective work has opened to me, and
there are many who oppose me.
—1 Corinthians 16:9

A month after we arrived in Guatemala, I and some
pastors riding with me were captured in the highlands
by guerrillas and threatened with execution. Two
months after our arrival, my father was the victim of a
kidnap attempt in front of our house mere hours after
he had landed in Guatemala City to visit us.

We began to wonder what we were doing there
and if we had gotten in over our heads. Immediately
following the second incident, our field director, Ray
Canfield, drove up to Guatemala City with his wife
to see how we were doing. They shared 1 Corinthians
16:9 with us. Ray told us, "You are taking on the enemy—he will fight. But God has work for you here.
Don't give up."

The next season of ministry proved to be exactly what Paul had described in his epistle to the
Corinthians: great harvesting and great opposition.

In the years since, we have *also* known periods of rest and renewal in the context of fruitful ministry; for those times of respite, we thank God. Yet those quiet years are less frequent than the others. One might almost conclude that the size of the harvest in a location is directly proportionate to the level of upheaval occurring in a society—or at least the opposition one encounters.

As a country, we have experienced a season of dislocation on several levels in governmental, social, and spiritual realms. Just as this kind of upheaval removed barriers that had hardened hearts to the gospel in Guatemala, might we see something similar take place among us?

Could it be that we will witness wide-open doors for effective work in our midst? Might God use the very circumstances that have stoked anxiety and despair to turn the hearts of many toward Jesus? What might that look like, and how can we best align ourselves with God's intentions?

When the larger world erupts and finds existing worldviews and philosophies unsatisfactory, will I be ready to give defense of the hope that is in me? (1 Peter 3:15)?

Enthusiasts

> At this point Festus interrupted Paul's defense. "You
> are out of your mind, Paul!" he shouted. "Your great
> learning is driving you insane."
> —Acts 26:24

In eighteenth century England, the traditional
Anglicans referred to Charles Wesley's upstart followers as "enthusiasts." It was not a compliment. They
viewed these passionate Christians as fanatics—as
both an annoyance and an embarrassment to society.

Such is the scandal of devotion. People are fine
with "religion" as long as it knows its place: observed
in private corners but making no pronouncements,
providing order to the annual civic calendar so we
know when to party.

Paul did not follow these rules—Jesus *definitely*
did not! They rocked the religious boat in Palestine
and eventually sank the imperial galley with their
insane suggestion that Jesus, not Caesar, deserves our
full devotion. The empire dealt with both of them the
only way it knew how.

Empires have not changed in two thousand years. Domesticated, toothless faith will always have a place at the society table; fearless faith will not.

We find ourselves in a liminal moment. "Nice religion" has lost the ability to influence society because the old accords have ended. States no longer need or want religious approval, and people bound by isolation and alienation find no meaning in religious moralism.

This is actually a marvelous moment in which to *be* the church. I refer to the community of men and women who confess Jesus as both Lord and Savior and who invite God to exercise authority in *every* area of their lives (Romans 12:1–2). Why? Precisely because the old systems (political, social, religious) have run their course, and we have something so much better than a system to offer: full citizenship in the kingdom of God! This is the kingdom that redeems, reconciles, and restores.

I am convinced of this: the unchurched will not be won by "nice" people. We have to become enthusiastic about our faith, about Jesus, about loving non-Christians—but not in romantic ways. We have to climb into their world and walk with them.

In Matthew 11:12, after the murder of John the Baptist, Jesus declared that the kingdom of God has already been subject to violence, "and violent people have been raiding it." The church that overcomes will

210

be Spirit-filled, grounded in Scripture, and fearless to proclaim the good news of Jesus with love and boldness.

What has God invited me to do that I have feared to obey because it might rock the boat? What might the first step of obedience require of me?